Claire BRETÉCHER

What a Life...

Frederick Muller Ltd
London SW19 7JZ

Published in Great Britain in 1982 by
Frederick Muller Ltd
Dataday House
Wimbledon, London SW19 7JZ
in association with Charles Herridge Ltd

ISBN 0 584 40000 4

Printed in England by
Devon Print Group, Exeter.

Jane

I could grow my hair long...

give contact lenses a try...

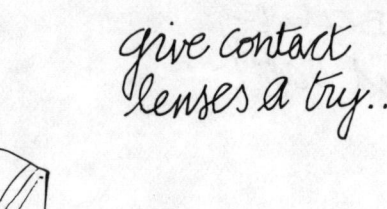

get THAT massaged...

tone up my muscles...
do a keep-fit course...
regular exercise...

get some clothes together... something laid back...

rent a studio or something like that...

find a job I can get into... some man with the same lifestyle...

then the hardest part would be over

I could really start LIVING

the glowing hearth

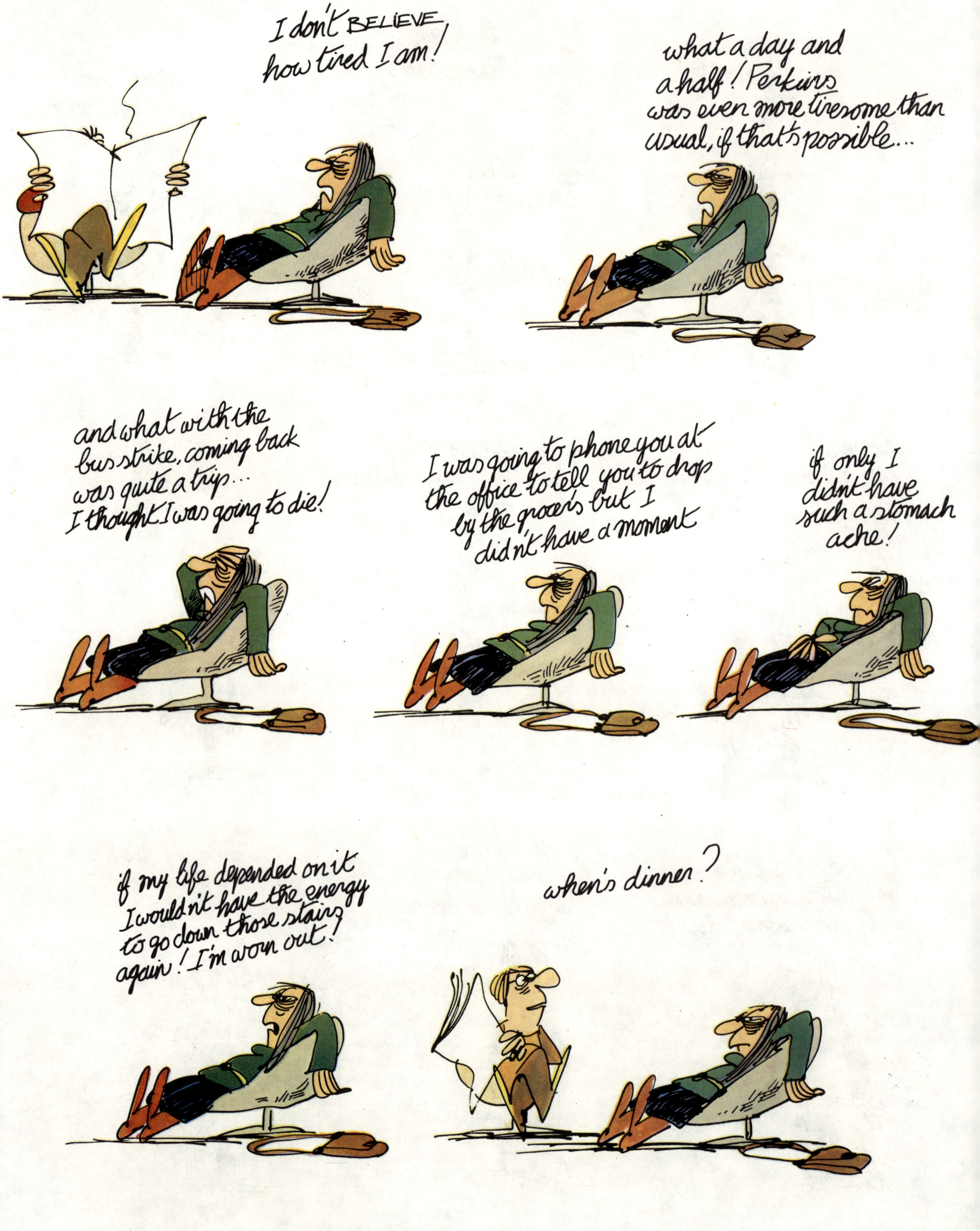
I don't BELIEVE how tired I am!
what a day and a half! Perkins was even more tiresome than usual, if that's possible...
and what with the bus strike, coming back was quite a trip... I thought I was going to die!
I was going to phone you at the office to tell you to drop by the grocer's but I didn't have a moment
if only I didn't have such a stomach ache!
if my life depended on it I wouldn't have the energy to go down those stairs again! I'm worn out!
when's dinner?

panic in Eden park

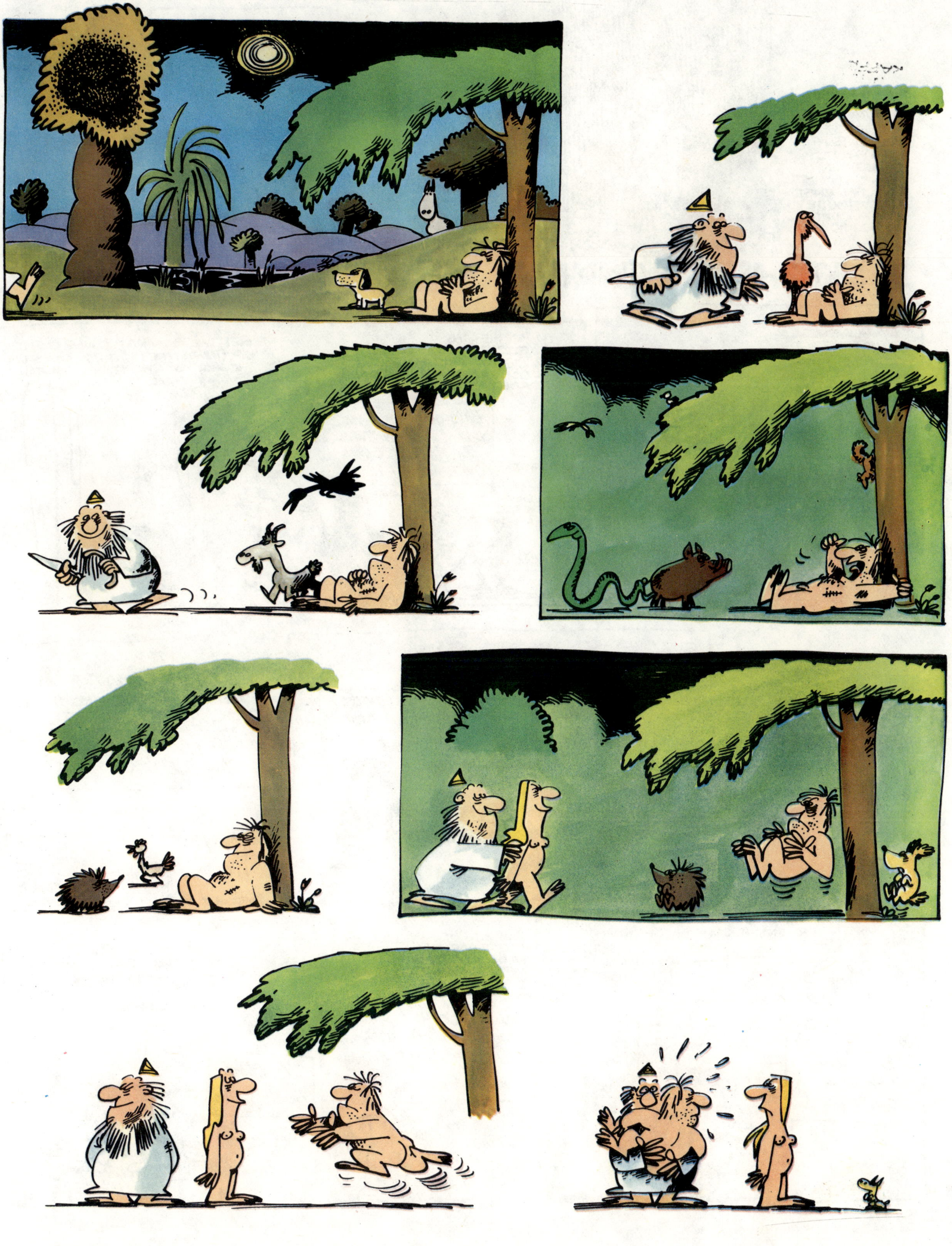

the photographer

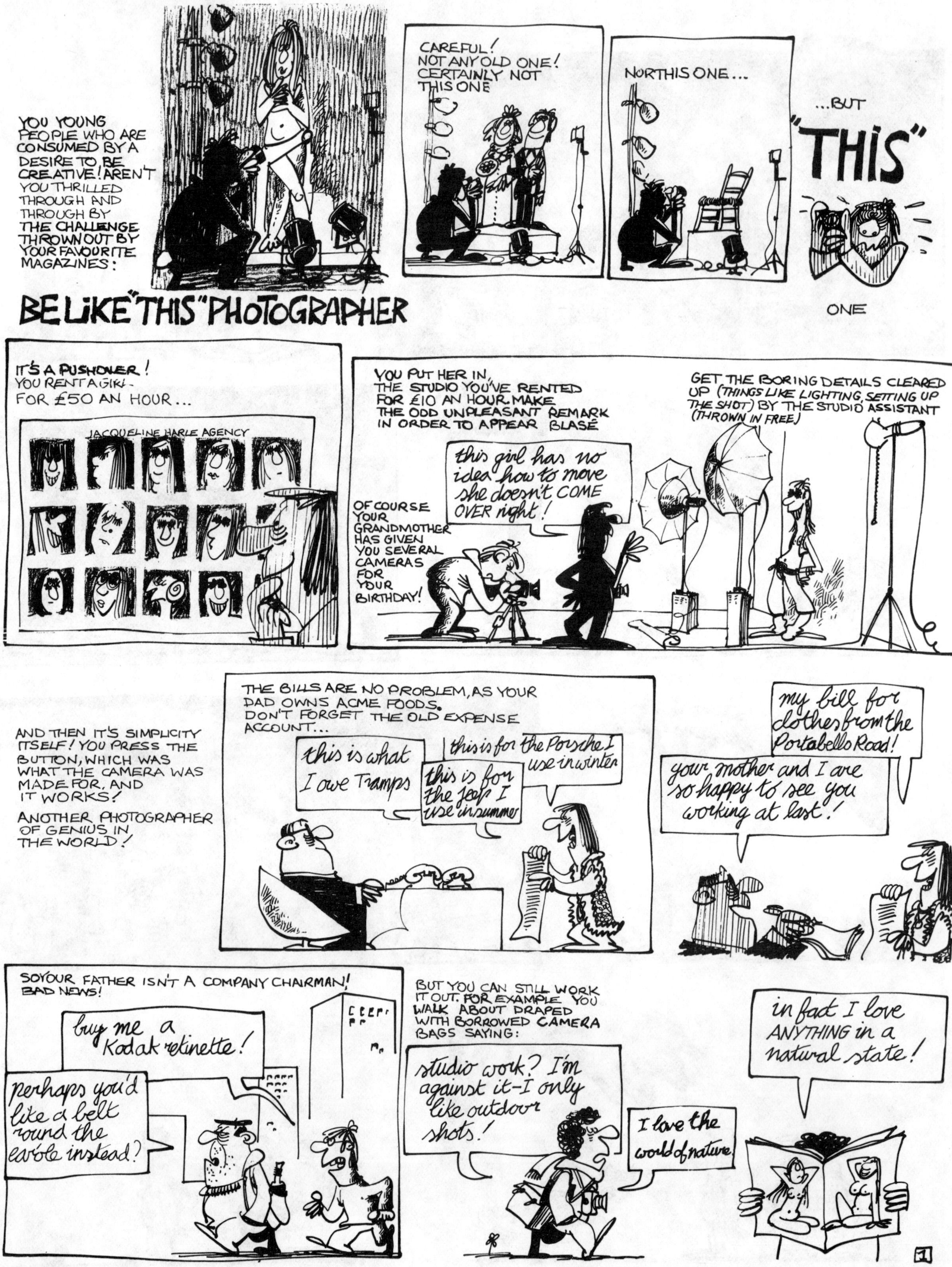

YOU YOUNG PEOPLE WHO ARE CONSUMED BY A DESIRE TO BE CREATIVE! AREN'T YOU THRILLED THROUGH AND THROUGH BY THE CHALLENGE THROWN OUT BY YOUR FAVOURITE MAGAZINES:
BE LIKE "THIS" PHOTOGRAPHER
CAREFUL! NOT ANY OLD ONE! CERTAINLY NOT THIS ONE
NOR THIS ONE...
...BUT "THIS" ONE
IT'S A PUSHOVER! YOU RENT A GIRL - FOR £50 AN HOUR...
JACQUELINE HARLE AGENCY
YOU PUT HER IN THE STUDIO YOU'VE RENTED FOR £10 AN HOUR. MAKE THE ODD UNPLEASANT REMARK IN ORDER TO APPEAR BLASÉ
this girl has no idea how to move she doesn't COME OVER right!
OF COURSE YOUR GRANDMOTHER HAS GIVEN YOU SEVERAL CAMERAS FOR YOUR BIRTHDAY!
GET THE BORING DETAILS CLEARED UP (THINGS LIKE LIGHTING, SETTING UP THE SHOT) BY THE STUDIO ASSISTANT (THROWN IN FREE)
AND THEN IT'S SIMPLICITY ITSELF! YOU PRESS THE BUTTON, WHICH WAS WHAT THE CAMERA WAS MADE FOR, AND IT WORKS!
ANOTHER PHOTOGRAPHER OF GENIUS IN THE WORLD!
THE BILLS ARE NO PROBLEM, AS YOUR DAD OWNS ACME FOODS. DON'T FORGET THE OLD EXPENSE ACCOUNT...
this is what I owe Tramps
this is for the Porsche I use in winter
this is for the jeep I use in summer
my bill for clothes from the Portabello Road!
your mother and I are so happy to see you working at last!
SO YOUR FATHER ISN'T A COMPANY CHAIRMAN! BAD NEWS!
buy me a Kodak retinette!
perhaps you'd like a belt round the earole instead?
BUT YOU CAN STILL WORK IT OUT. FOR EXAMPLE YOU WALK ABOUT DRAPED WITH BORROWED CAMERA BAGS SAYING:
studio work? I'm against it - I only like outdoor shots!
I love the world of nature
in fact I love ANYTHING in a natural state!

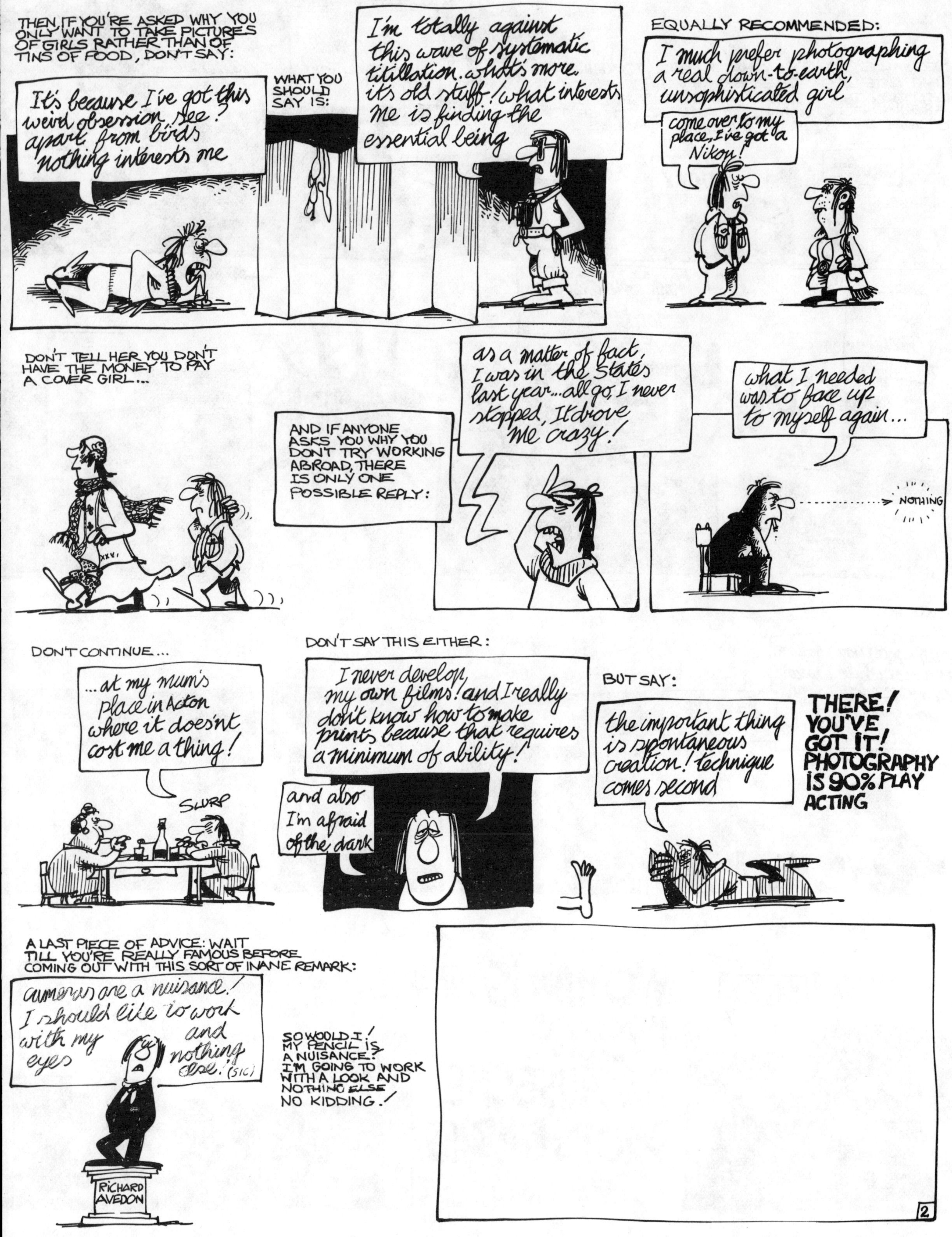

THEN, IF YOU'RE ASKED WHY YOU ONLY WANT TO TAKE PICTURES OF GIRLS RATHER THAN OF TINS OF FOOD, DON'T SAY:
It's because I've got this weird obsession see? apart from birds nothing interests me
WHAT YOU SHOULD SAY IS:
I'm totally against this wave of systematic titillation.. what's more, it's old stuff! what interests me is finding the essential being
EQUALLY RECOMMENDED:
I much prefer photographing a real down-to-earth, unsophisticated girl
come over to my place, I've got a Nikon!
DON'T TELL HER YOU DON'T HAVE THE MONEY TO PAY A COVER GIRL...
AND IF ANYONE ASKS YOU WHY YOU DON'T TRY WORKING ABROAD, THERE IS ONLY ONE POSSIBLE REPLY:
as a matter of fact, I was in the States last year... all go, I never stopped, It drove me crazy!
what I needed was to face up to myself again...
NOTHING
DON'T CONTINUE...
...at my mum's place in Acton where it doesn't cost me a thing!
SLURP
DON'T SAY THIS EITHER:
I never develop my own films! and I really don't know how to make prints because that requires a minimum of ability!
and also I'm afraid of the dark
BUT SAY:
the important thing is spontaneous creation! technique comes second
THERE! YOU'VE GOT IT! PHOTOGRAPHY IS 90% PLAY ACTING
A LAST PIECE OF ADVICE: WAIT TILL YOU'RE REALLY FAMOUS BEFORE COMING OUT WITH THIS SORT OF INANE REMARK:
cameras are a nuisance! I should like to work with my eyes and nothing else! (SIC)
RICHARD AVEDON
SO WOULD I! MY PENCIL IS A NUISANCE! I'M GOING TO WORK WITH A LOOK AND NOTHING ELSE NO KIDDING!

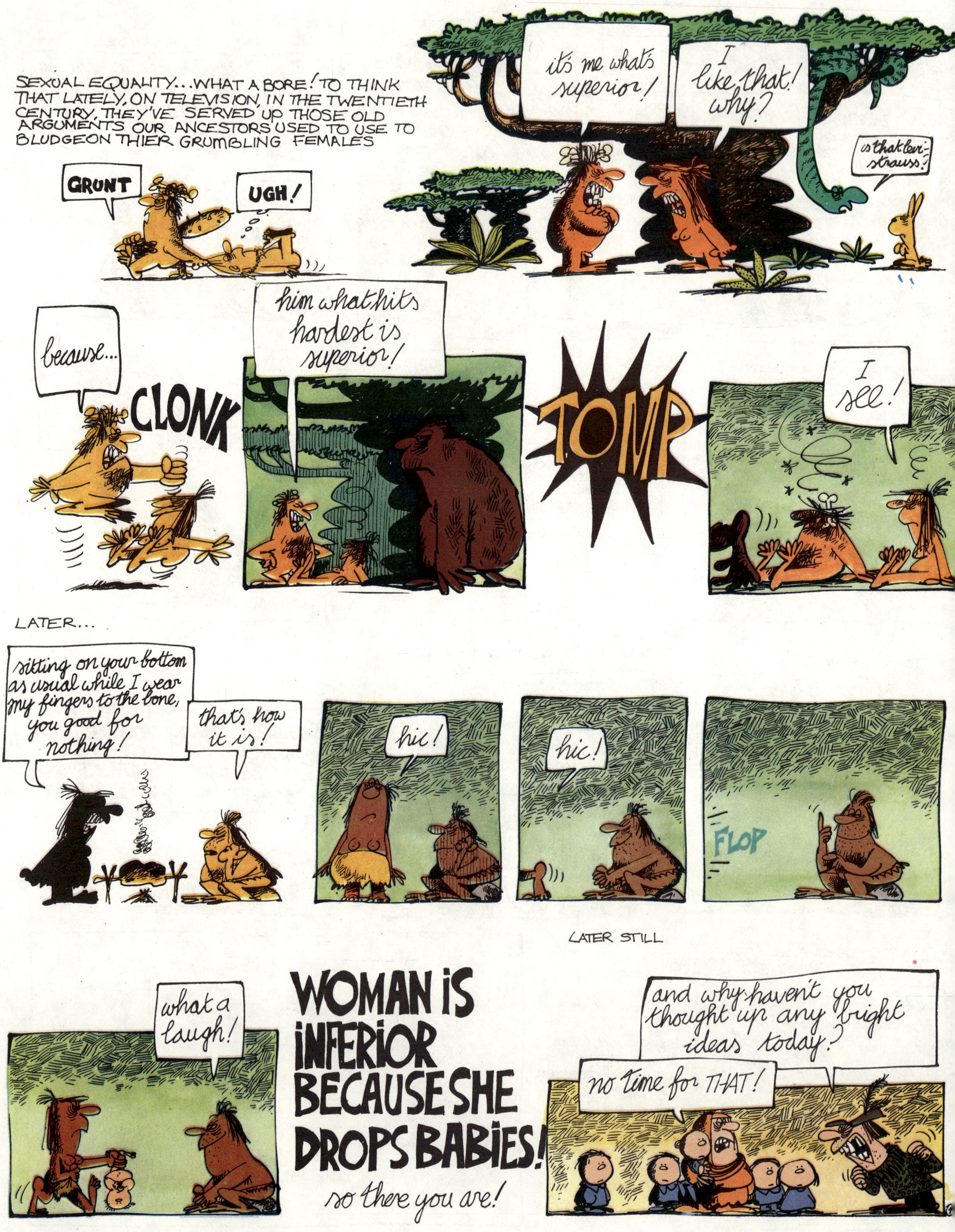
SEXUAL EQUALITY... WHAT A BORE! TO THINK THAT LATELY, ON TELEVISION, IN THE TWENTIETH CENTURY, THEY'VE SERVED UP THOSE OLD ARGUMENTS OUR ANCESTORS USED TO USE TO BLUDGEON THIER GRUMBLING FEMALES
GRUNT
UGH!
it's me what's superior!
I like that! why?
is that levi-strauss?
because...
CLONK
him what hits hardest is superior!
TOMP
I see!
LATER...
sitting on your bottom as usual while I wear my fingers to the bone, you good for nothing!
that's how it is!
hic!
hic!
FLOP
LATER STILL
what a laugh!
WOMAN IS INFERIOR BECAUSE SHE DROPS BABIES!
so there you are!
and why haven't you thought up any bright ideas today?
no time for THAT!

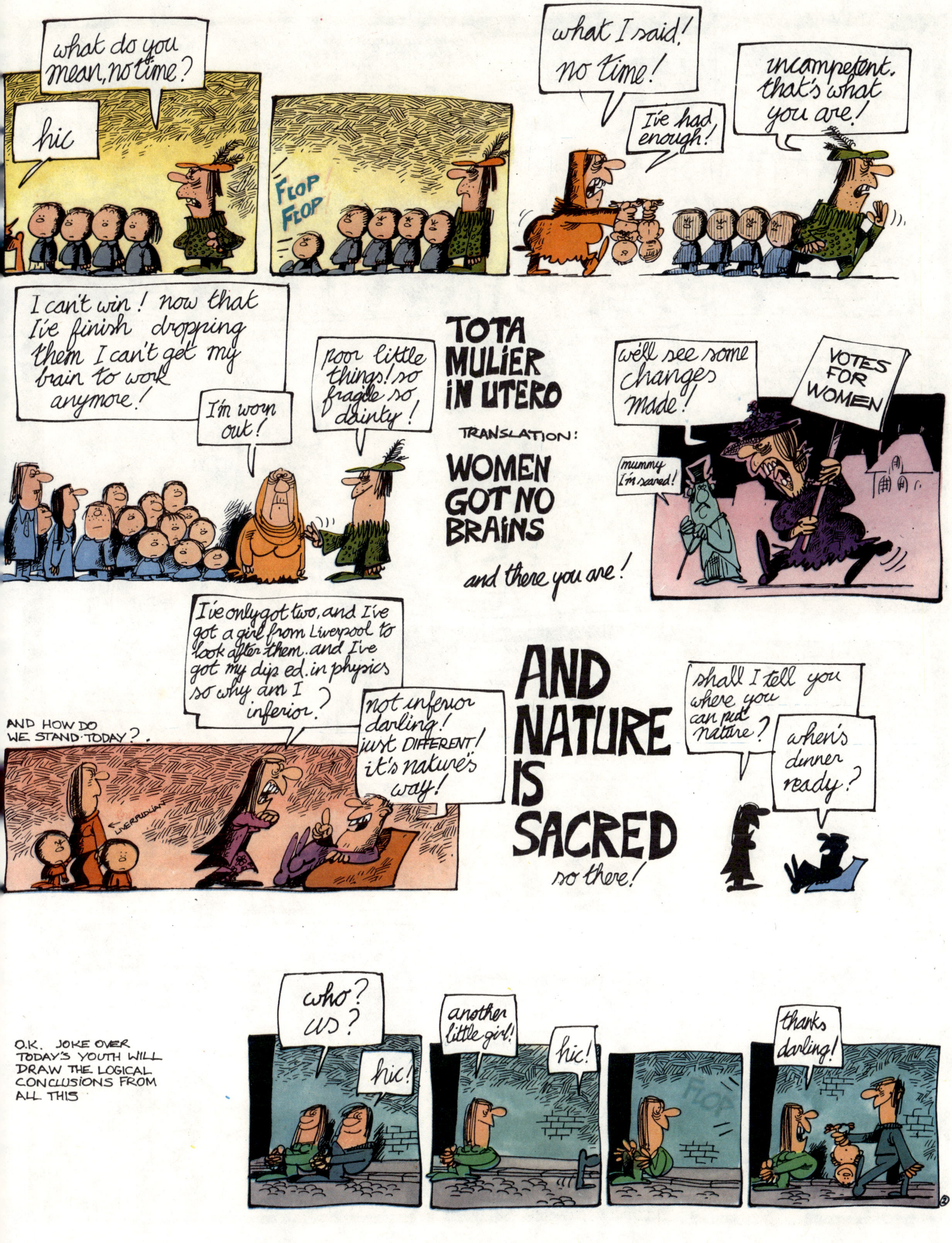

what do you mean, no time?
hic
FLOP FLOP
what I said! no time!
I've had enough!
incampetent. that's what you are!
I can't win! now that I've finish dropping them I can't get my brain to work anymore!
I'm worn out!
poor little things! so fragile so dainty!
TOTA MULIER IN UTERO
TRANSLATION:
WOMEN GOT NO BRAINS
and there you are!
we'll see some changes made!
VOTES FOR WOMEN
mummy I'm scared!
AND HOW DO WE STAND TODAY?
I've only got two, and I've got a girl from Liverpool to look after them. and I've got my dip ed. in physics so why am I inferior?
LIVERPUDLIAN
not inferior darling! just DIFFERENT! it's nature's way!
AND NATURE IS SACRED
so there!
shall I tell you where you can put nature?
when's dinner ready?
O.K. JOKE OVER TODAY'S YOUTH WILL DRAW THE LOGICAL CONCLUSIONS FROM ALL THIS
who? us?
hic!
another little girl!
hic!
FLOP
thanks darling!

Mrs Parker's great adventure

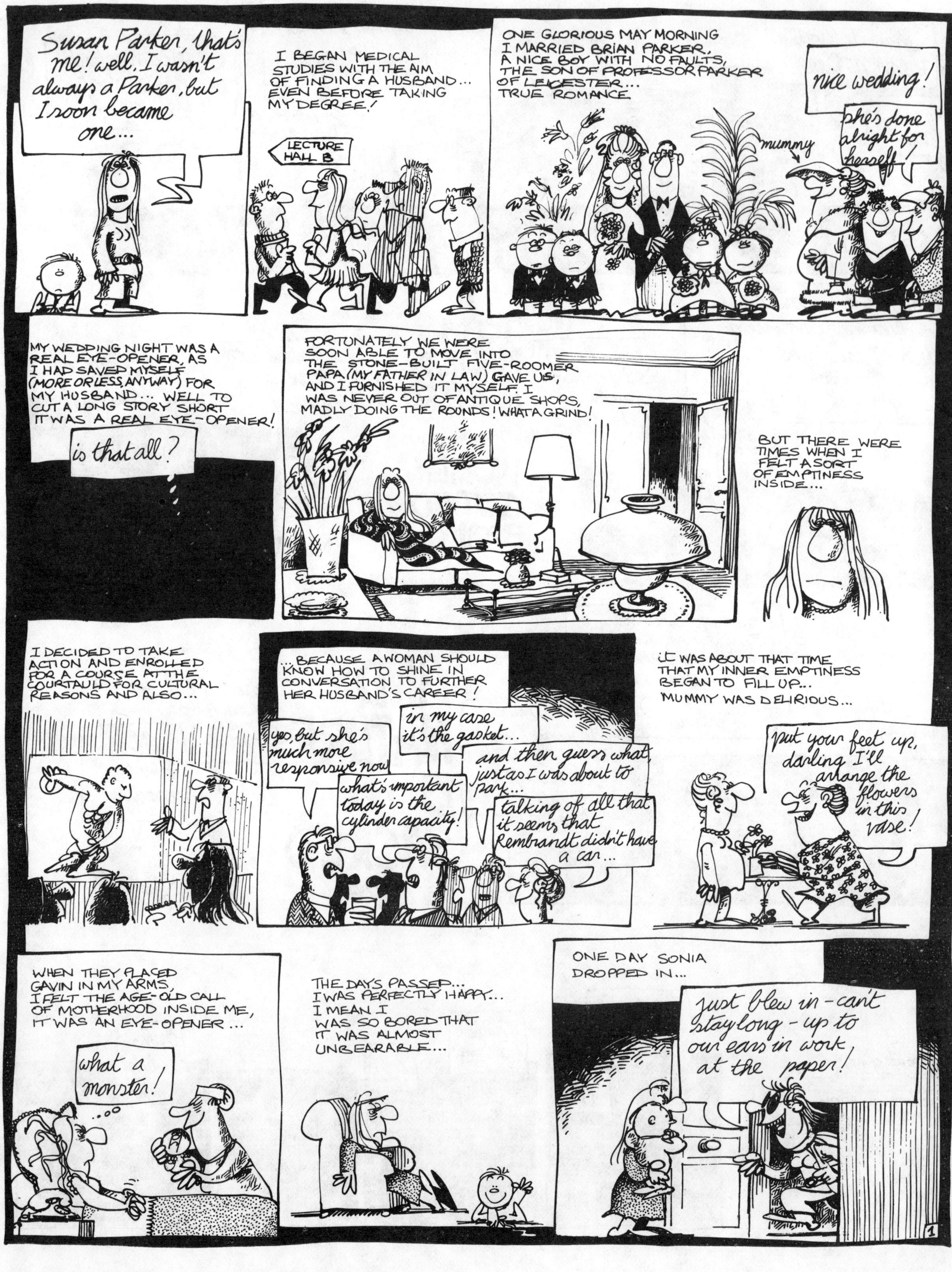

Susan Parker, that's me! well, I wasn't always a Parker, but I soon became one...
I BEGAN MEDICAL STUDIES WITH THE AIM OF FINDING A HUSBAND... EVEN BEFORE TAKING MY DEGREE!
LECTURE HALL B
ONE GLORIOUS MAY MORNING I MARRIED BRIAN PARKER, A NICE BOY WITH NO FAULTS, THE SON OF PROFESSOR PARKER OF LEICESTER... TRUE ROMANCE
nice wedding!
she's done alright for herself!
mummy
MY WEDDING NIGHT WAS A REAL EYE-OPENER, AS I HAD SAVED MYSELF (MORE OR LESS, ANYWAY) FOR MY HUSBAND... WELL TO CUT A LONG STORY SHORT IT WAS A REAL EYE-OPENER!
is that all?
FORTUNATELY WE WERE SOON ABLE TO MOVE INTO THE STONE-BUILT FIVE-ROOMER PAPA (MY FATHER IN LAW) GAVE US, AND I FURNISHED IT MYSELF. I WAS NEVER OUT OF ANTIQUE SHOPS, MADLY DOING THE ROUNDS! WHAT A GRIND!
BUT THERE WERE TIMES WHEN I FELT A SORT OF EMPTINESS INSIDE...
I DECIDED TO TAKE ACTION AND ENROLLED FOR A COURSE AT THE COURTAULD FOR CULTURAL REASONS AND ALSO...
...BECAUSE A WOMAN SHOULD KNOW HOW TO SHINE IN CONVERSATION TO FURTHER HER HUSBAND'S CAREER!
yes, but she's much more responsive now
in my case it's the gasket...
what's important today is the cylinder capacity!
and then guess what, just as I was about to park...
talking of all that it seems that Rembrandt didn't have a car...
IT WAS ABOUT THAT TIME THAT MY INNER EMPTINESS BEGAN TO FILL UP... MUMMY WAS DELIRIOUS...
put your feet up, darling. I'll arrange the flowers in this vase!
WHEN THEY PLACED GAVIN IN MY ARMS, I FELT THE AGE-OLD CALL OF MOTHERHOOD INSIDE ME, IT WAS AN EYE-OPENER...
what a monster!
THE DAYS PASSED... I WAS PERFECTLY HAPPY... I MEAN I WAS SO BORED THAT IT WAS ALMOST UNBEARABLE...
ONE DAY SONIA DROPPED IN...
just blew in - can't stay long - up to our ears in work at the paper!
1

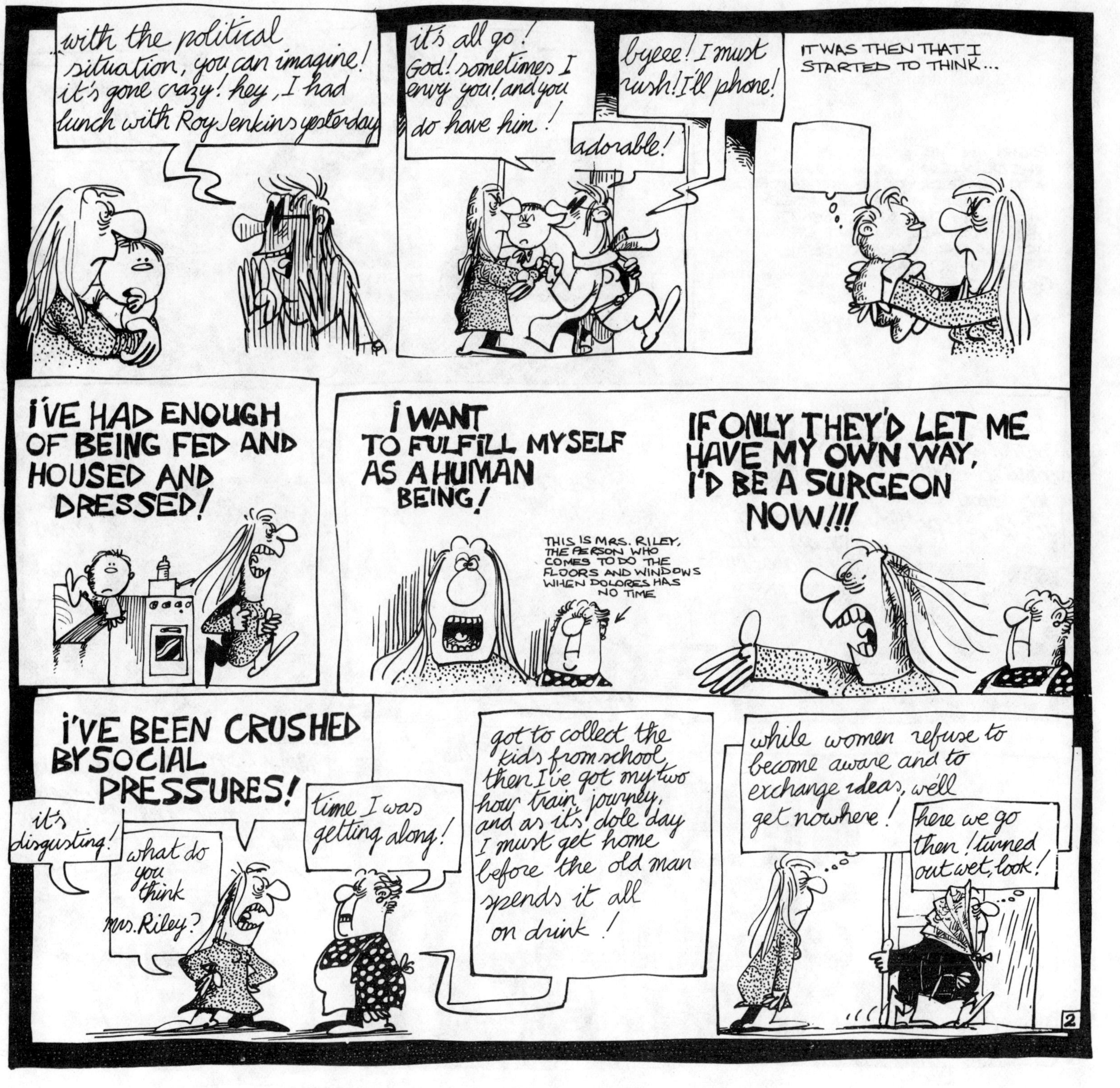
...with the political situation, you can imagine! it's gone crazy! hey, I had lunch with Roy Jenkins yesterday
it's all go! God! sometimes I envy you! and you do have him!
adorable!
byeee! I must rush! I'll phone!
IT WAS THEN THAT I STARTED TO THINK...
I'VE HAD ENOUGH OF BEING FED AND HOUSED AND DRESSED!
I WANT TO FULFILL MYSELF AS A HUMAN BEING!
THIS IS MRS. RILEY, THE PERSON WHO COMES TO DO THE FLOORS AND WINDOWS WHEN DOLORES HAS NO TIME
IF ONLY THEY'D LET ME HAVE MY OWN WAY, I'D BE A SURGEON NOW!!!
I'VE BEEN CRUSHED BY SOCIAL PRESSURES!
it's disgusting!
what do you think Mrs. Riley?
time I was getting along!
got to collect the kids from school, then I've got my two hour train journey, and as it's dole day I must get home before the old man spends it all on drink!
while women refuse to become aware and to exchange ideas, we'll get nowhere!
here we go then! turned out wet, look!
2

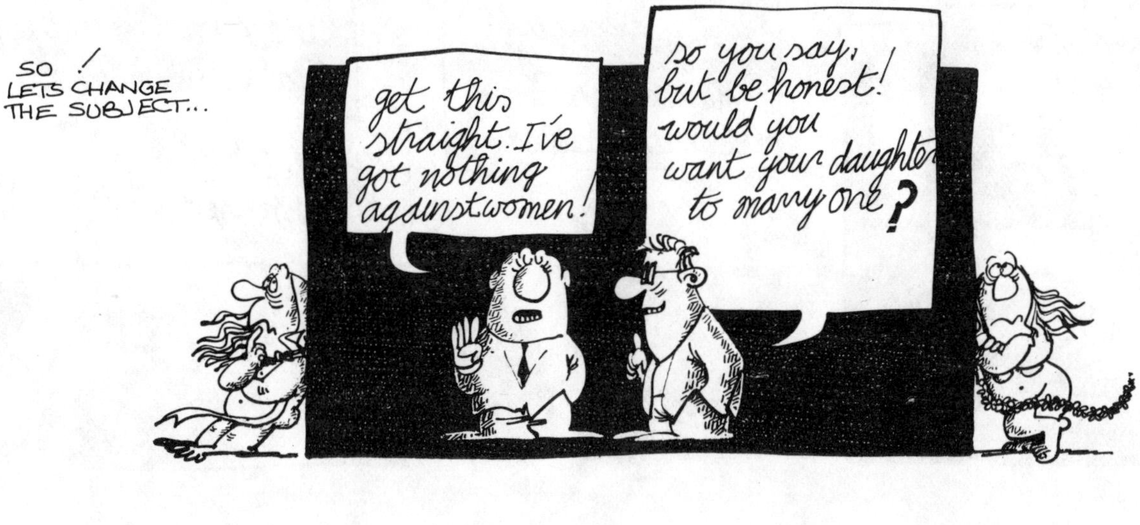
SO! LETS CHANGE THE SUBJECT...
get this straight. I've got nothing against women!
so you say, but be honest! would you want your daughter to marry one?

RIGHT IN THE HEART OF THE OLD TOWN, GAVIN STEVENS, A TALENTED YOUNG INTERIOR DESIGNER, HAS RENOVATED HIS OWN ATTIC APARTMENT, USING A SMALL AMOUNT OF MONEY AND A GREAT DEAL OF INGENUITY AND GOOD TASTE...

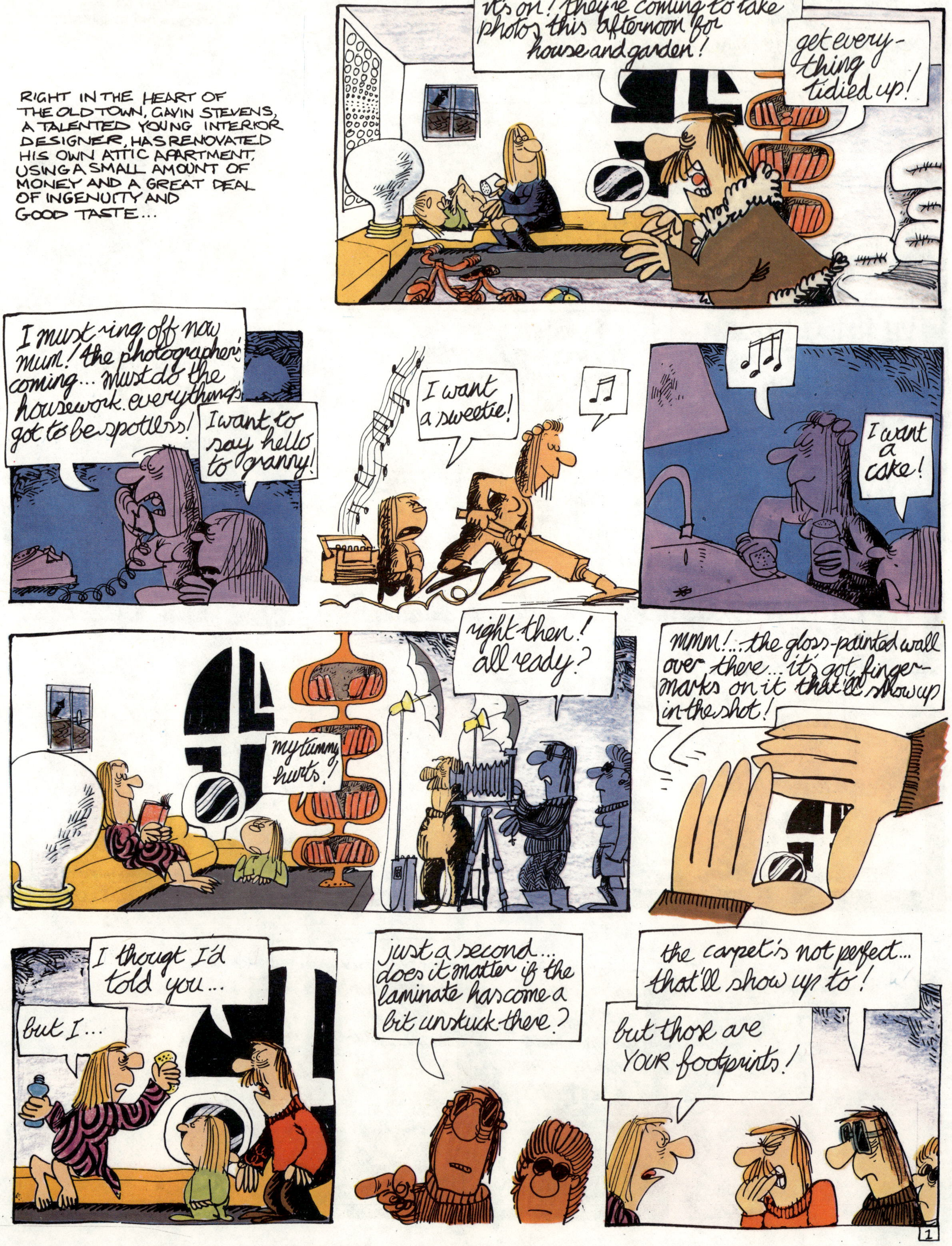
it's on! they're coming to take photos this afternoon for house and garden!
get every-thing tidied up!
I must ring off now mum! the photographer's coming... must do the housework. everything's got to be spotless!
I want to say hello to granny!
I want a sweetie!
I want a cake!
right then! all ready?
my tummy hurts!
mmm!... the gloss-painted wall over there... it's got finger-marks on it that'll show up in the shot!
I thougt I'd told you...
but I...
just a second... does it matter if the laminate has come a bit unstuck there?
the carpet's not perfect... that'll show up to!
but those are YOUR footprints!

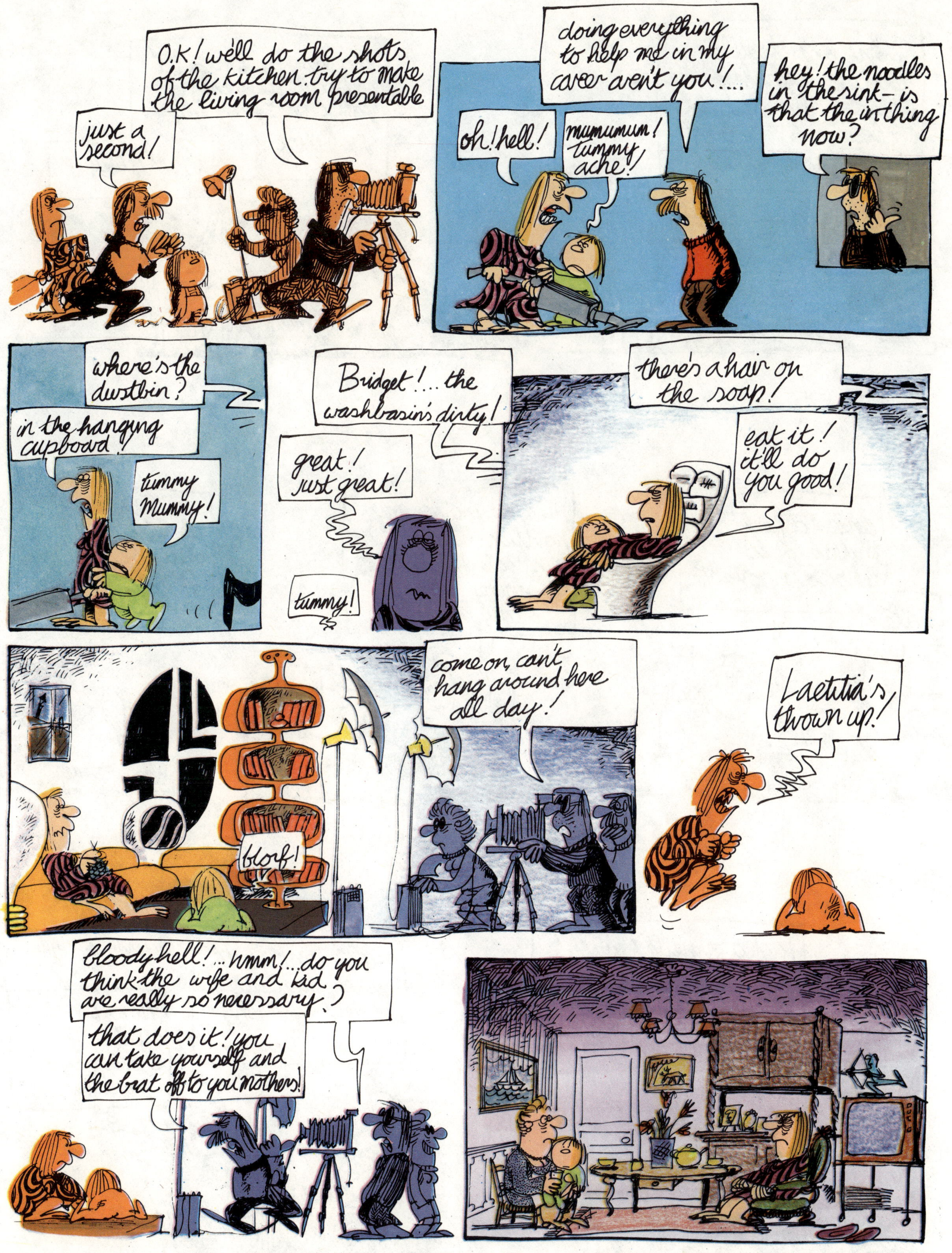

O.K! we'll do the shots of the kitchen: try to make the living room presentable
just a second!
doing everything to help me in my career aren't you!...
oh! hell!
mumumum! tummy ache!
hey! the noodles in the sink– is that the in thing now?
where's the dustbin?
in the hanging cupboard!
tummy Mummy!
Bridget!... the washbasin's dirty!
great! just great!
tummy!
there's a hair on the soap!
eat it! it'll do you good!
come on, can't hang around here all day!
blorf!
Laetitia's thrown up!
bloody hell!... hmm!... do you think the wife and kid are really so necessary?
that does it! you can take yourself and the brat off to you mothers!

let's do some thinking

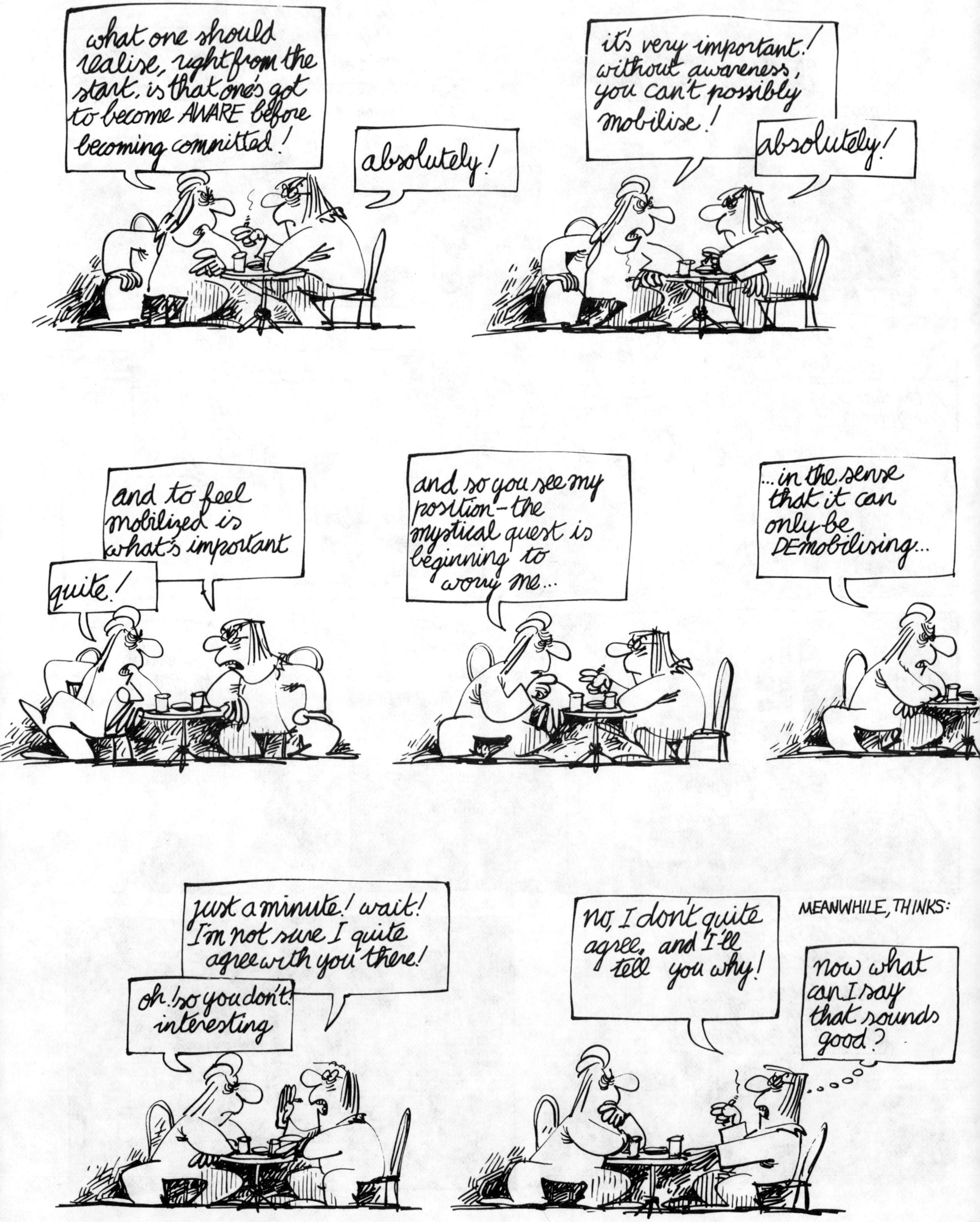
what one should realise, right from the start, is that one's got to become AWARE before becoming committed!
absolutely!
it's very important! without awareness, you can't possibly mobilise!
absolutely!
and to feel mobilized is what's important
quite!
and so you see my position – the mystical quest is beginning to worry me...
...in the sense that it can only be DEmobilising...
just a minute! wait! I'm not sure I quite agree with you there!
oh! so you don't! interesting
no, I don't quite agree, and I'll tell you why!
MEANWHILE, THINKS:
now what can I say that sounds good?

bitter moments

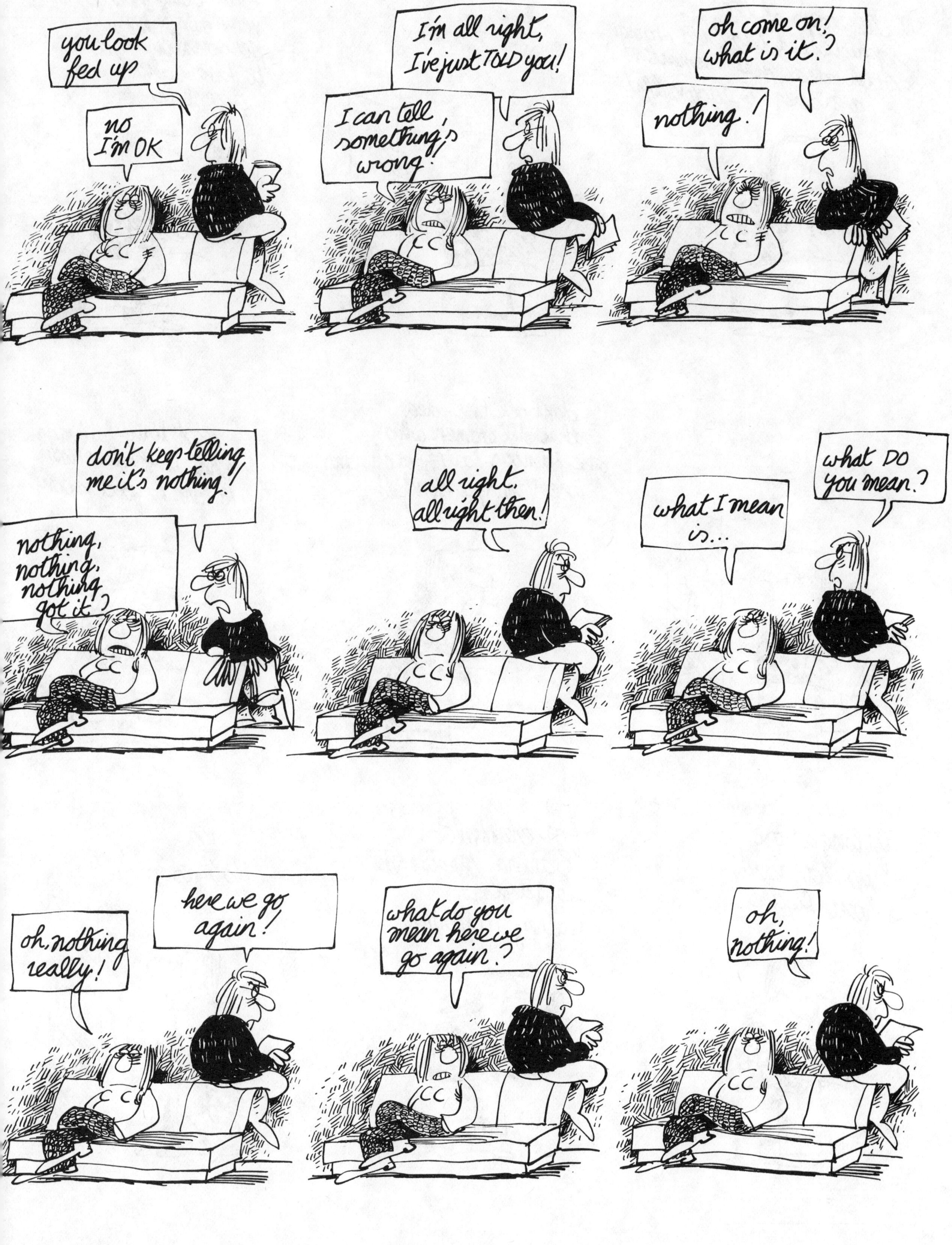

you look fed up
no I'M OK
I can tell, something's wrong!
I'm all right, I've just TOLD you!
oh come on! what is it?
nothing!
don't keep telling me it's nothing!
nothing, nothing, nothing got it?
all right, all right then!
what I mean is...
what DO you mean?
oh, nothing really!
here we go again!
what do you mean here we go again?
oh, nothing!

my problem

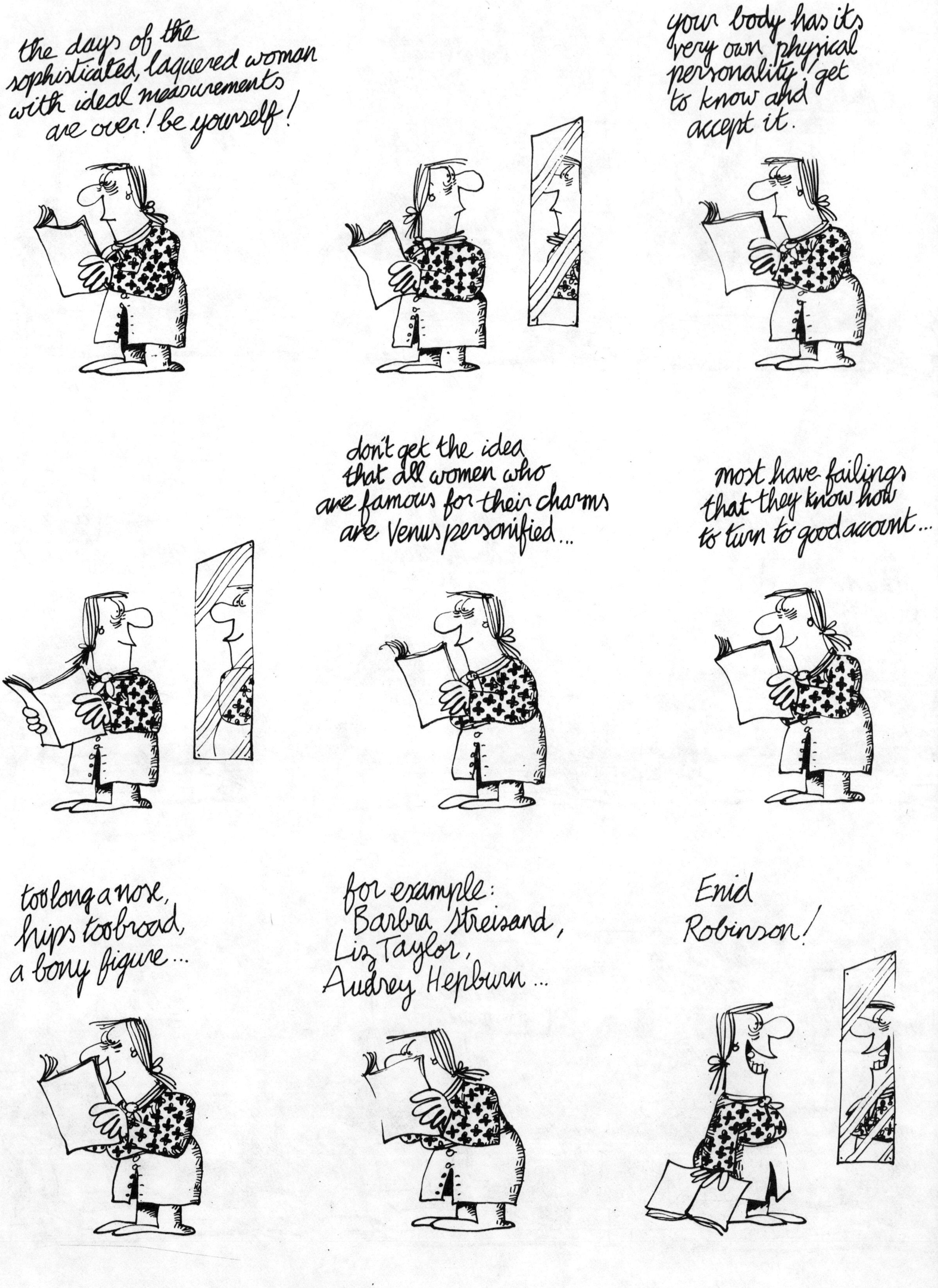
the days of the sophisticated, laquered woman with ideal measurements are over! be yourself!
your body has its very own physical personality! get to know and accept it.
don't get the idea that all women who are famous for their charms are Venus personified...
most have failings that they know how to turn to good account...
too long a nose, hips too broad, a bony figure...
for example: Barbra Streisand, Liz Taylor, Audrey Hepburn...
Enid Robinson!

the brick wall

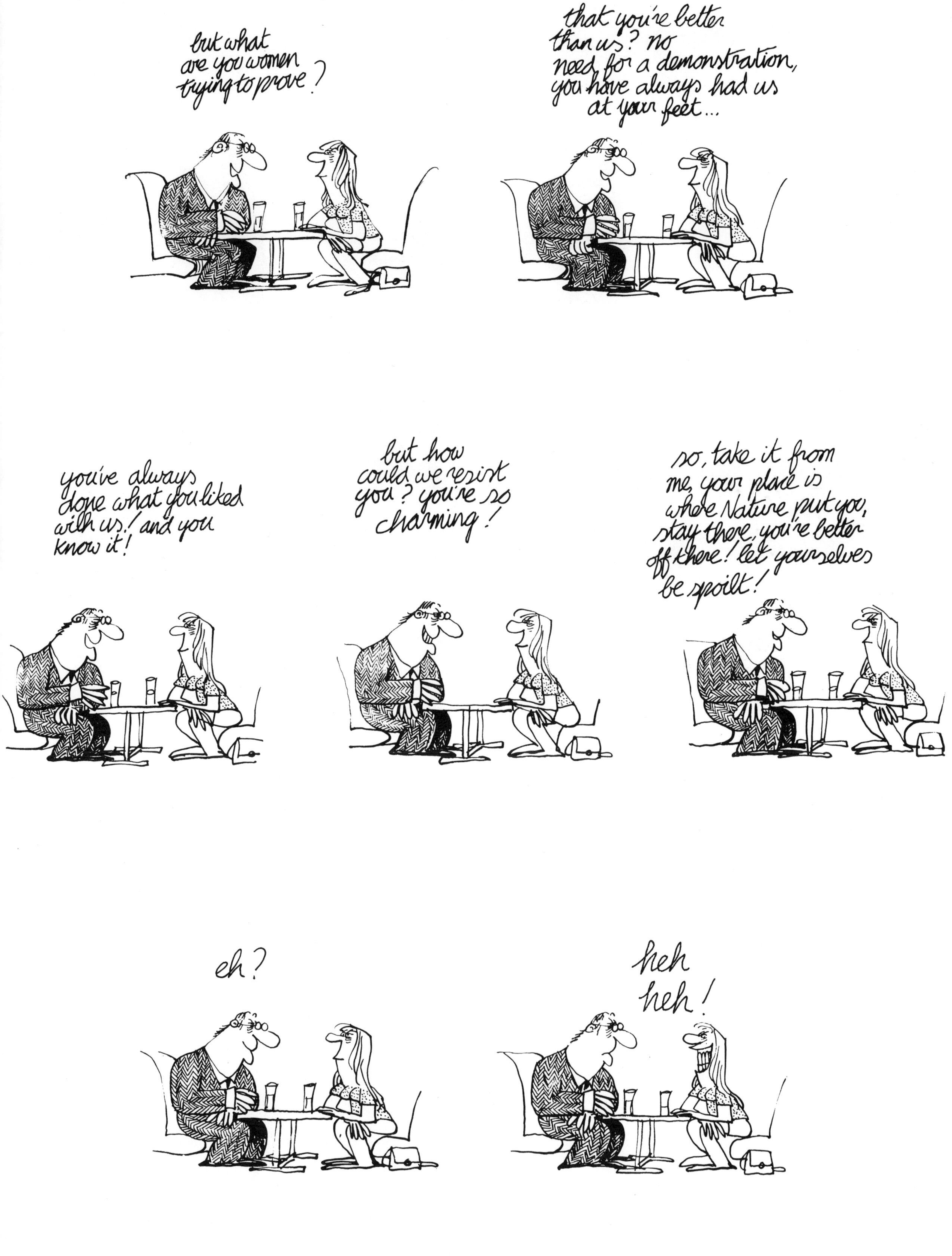

but what are you women trying to prove?
that you're better than us? no need for a demonstration, you have always had us at your feet...
you've always done what you liked with us! and you know it!
but how could we resist you? you're so charming!
so, take it from me, your place is where Nature put you, stay there, you're better off there! let yourselves be spoilt!
eh?
heh heh!

the elderly chairman

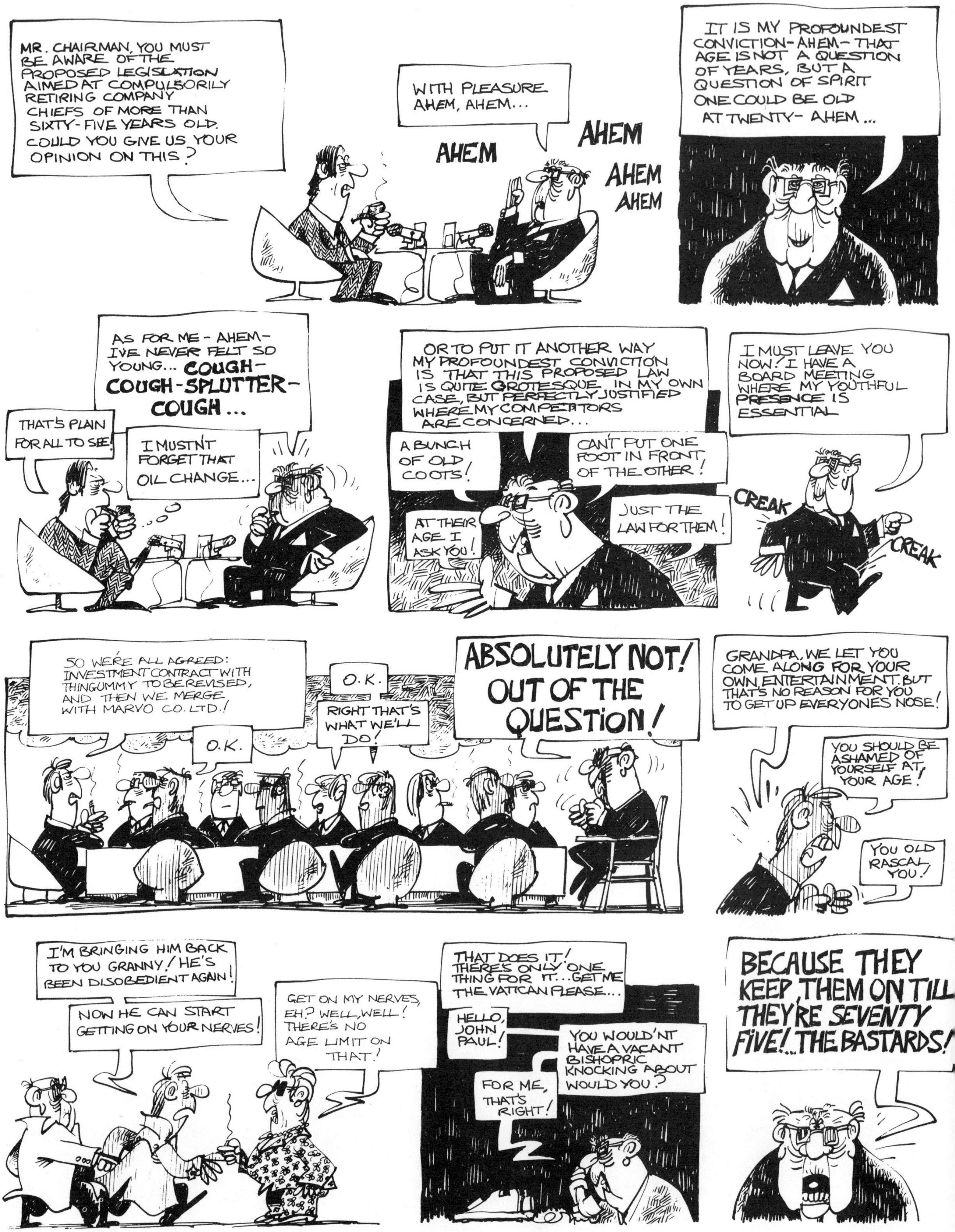
MR. CHAIRMAN, YOU MUST BE AWARE OF THE PROPOSED LEGISLATION AIMED AT COMPULSORILY RETIRING COMPANY CHIEFS OF MORE THAN SIXTY-FIVE YEARS OLD. COULD YOU GIVE US YOUR OPINION ON THIS?
WITH PLEASURE AHEM, AHEM...
AHEM
AHEM
AHEM
AHEM
IT IS MY PROFOUNDEST CONVICTION - AHEM - THAT AGE IS NOT A QUESTION OF YEARS, BUT A QUESTION OF SPIRIT ONE COULD BE OLD AT TWENTY - AHEM ...
AS FOR ME - AHEM - I'VE NEVER FELT SO YOUNG... COUGH - COUGH - SPLUTTER - COUGH ...
THAT'S PLAIN FOR ALL TO SEE!
I MUSTN'T FORGET THAT OIL CHANGE...
OR TO PUT IT ANOTHER WAY MY PROFOUNDEST CONVICTION IS THAT THIS PROPOSED LAW IS QUITE GROTESQUE IN MY OWN CASE, BUT PERFECTLY JUSTIFIED WHERE MY COMPETITORS ARE CONCERNED...
A BUNCH OF OLD COOTS!
CAN'T PUT ONE FOOT IN FRONT OF THE OTHER!
AT THEIR AGE I ASK YOU!
JUST THE LAW FOR THEM!
I MUST LEAVE YOU NOW! I HAVE A BOARD MEETING WHERE MY YOUTHFUL PRESENCE IS ESSENTIAL
CREAK
CREAK
SO WE'RE ALL AGREED: INVESTMENT CONTRACT WITH THINGUMMY TO BE REVISED, AND THEN WE MERGE WITH MARVO CO. LTD.!
O.K.
O.K.
RIGHT THAT'S WHAT WE'LL DO!
ABSOLUTELY NOT! OUT OF THE QUESTION!
GRANDPA, WE LET YOU COME ALONG FOR YOUR OWN ENTERTAINMENT. BUT THAT'S NO REASON FOR YOU TO GET UP EVERYONES NOSE!
YOU SHOULD BE ASHAMED OF YOURSELF AT YOUR AGE!
YOU OLD RASCAL YOU!
I'M BRINGING HIM BACK TO YOU GRANNY! HE'S BEEN DISOBEDIENT AGAIN!
NOW HE CAN START GETTING ON YOUR NERVES!
GET ON MY NERVES, EH? WELL, WELL! THERE'S NO AGE LIMIT ON THAT!
THAT DOES IT! THERE'S ONLY ONE THING FOR IT... GET ME THE VATICAN PLEASE...
HELLO, JOHN PAUL!
YOU WOULD'NT HAVE A VACANT BISHOPRIC KNOCKING ABOUT WOULD YOU?
FOR ME, THAT'S RIGHT!
BECAUSE THEY KEEP THEM ON TILL THEY'RE SEVENTY FIVE!... THE BASTARDS!

long days

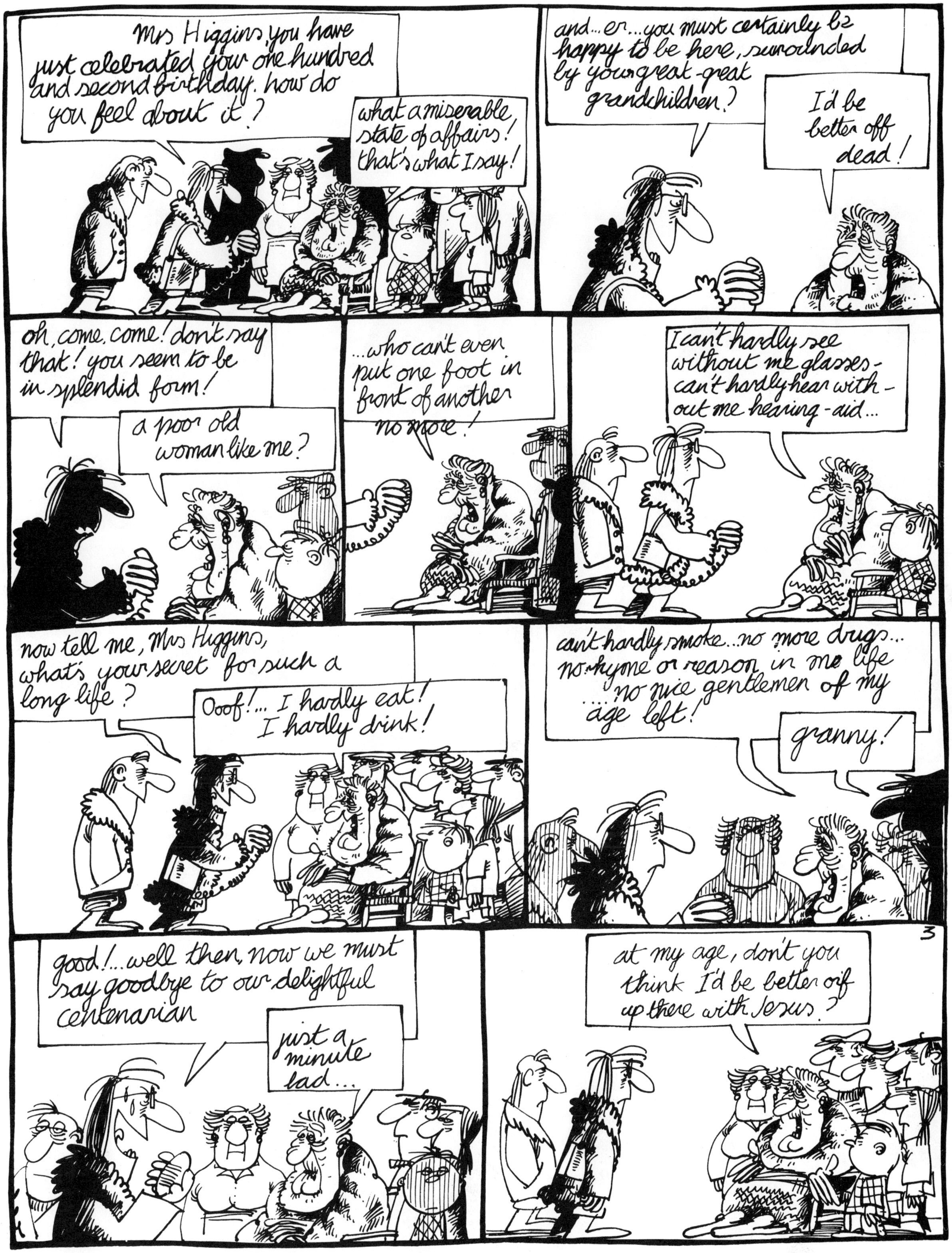
Mrs Higgins, you have just celebrated your one hundred and second birthday. how do you feel about it?
what a miserable state of affairs! that's what I say!
and... er... you must certainly be happy to be here, surrounded by your great-great grandchildren?
I'd be better off dead!
oh, come, come! don't say that! you seem to be in splendid form!
a poor old woman like me?
...who can't even put one foot in front of another no more!
I can't hardly see without me glasses - can't hardly hear without me hearing-aid...
now tell me, Mrs Higgins, what's your secret for such a long life?
Ooof!... I hardly eat! I hardly drink!
can't hardly smoke... no more drugs... no rhyme or reason in me life ... no nice gentlemen of my age left!
granny!
good!... well then, now we must say goodbye to our delightful centenarian
just a minute lad...
at my age, don't you think I'd be better off up there with Jesus?
3

introduction to French poetry

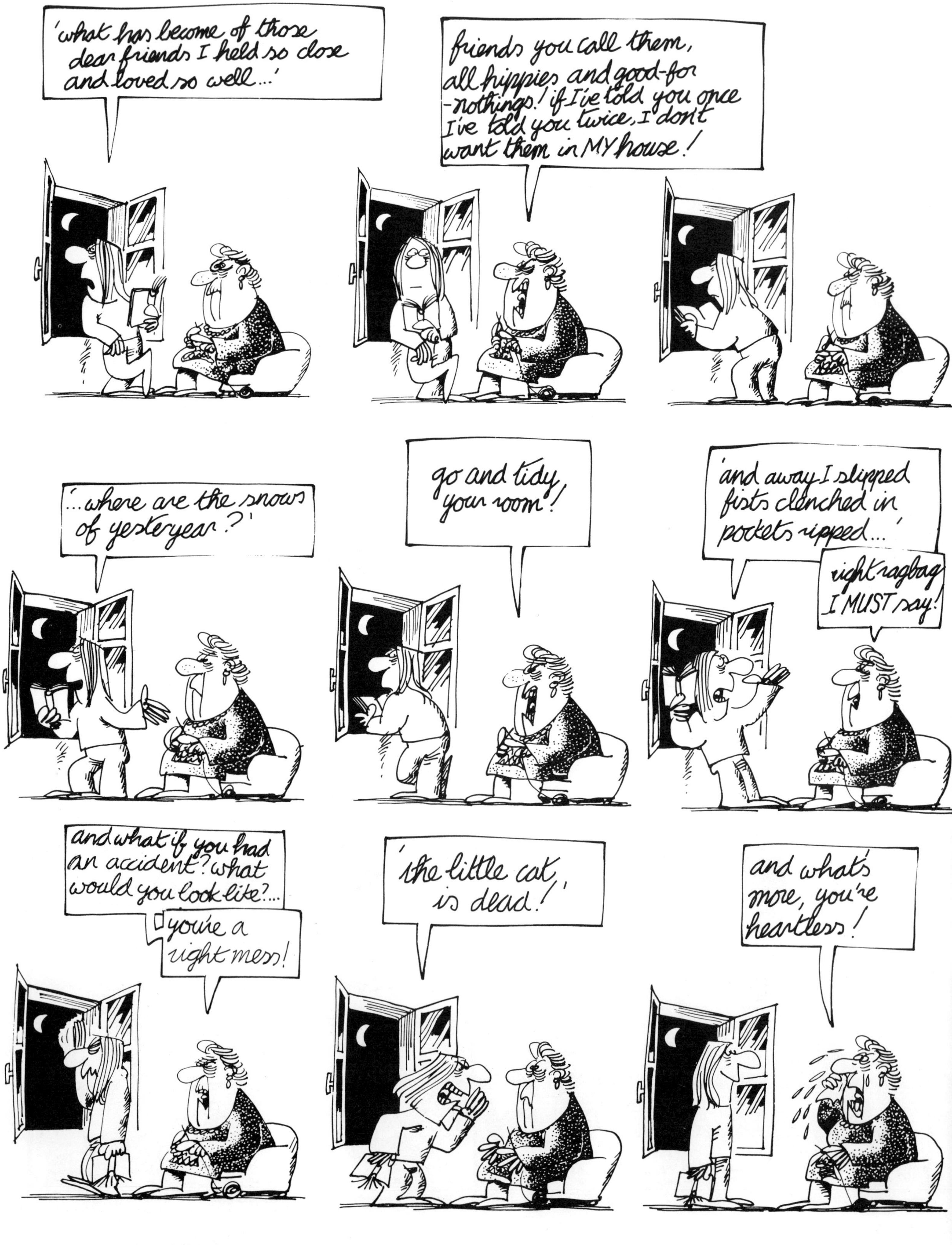
'what has become of those dear friends I held so close and loved so well...'
friends you call them, all hippies and good-for-nothings! if I've told you once I've told you twice, I don't want them in MY house!
'...where are the snows of yesteryear?'
go and tidy your room!
'and away I slipped fists clenched in pockets ripped...'
right ragbag I MUST say!
and what if you had an accident? what would you look like?...
you're a right mess!
'the little cat is dead!'
and what's more, you're heartless!

bellyachers

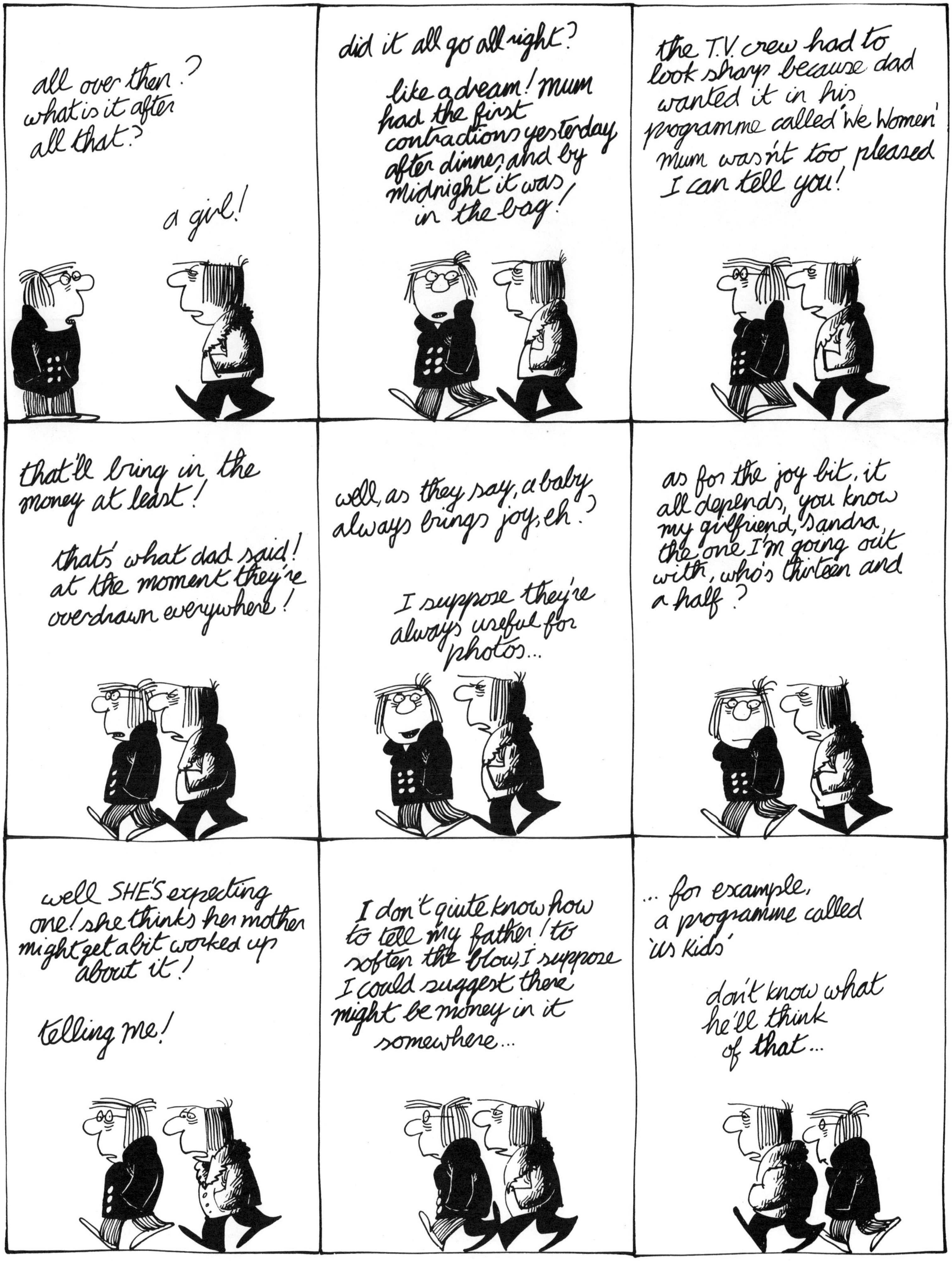

all over then? what is it after all that?
a girl!
did it all go all right?
like a dream! mum had the first contractions yesterday after dinner, and by midnight it was in the bag!
the T.V. crew had to look sharp because dad wanted it in his programme called 'We Women'. mum wasn't too pleased I can tell you!
that'll bring in the money at least!
that's what dad said! at the moment they're overdrawn everywhere!
well, as they say, a baby always brings joy, eh?
I suppose they're always useful for photos...
as for the joy bit, it all depends, you know my girlfriend, Sandra, the one I'm going out with, who's thirteen and a half?
well SHE'S expecting one! she thinks her mother might get a bit worked up about it!
telling me!
I don't quite know how to tell my father! to soften the blow, I suppose I could suggest there might be money in it somewhere...
... for example, a programme called 'Us Kids'
don't know what he'll think of that...

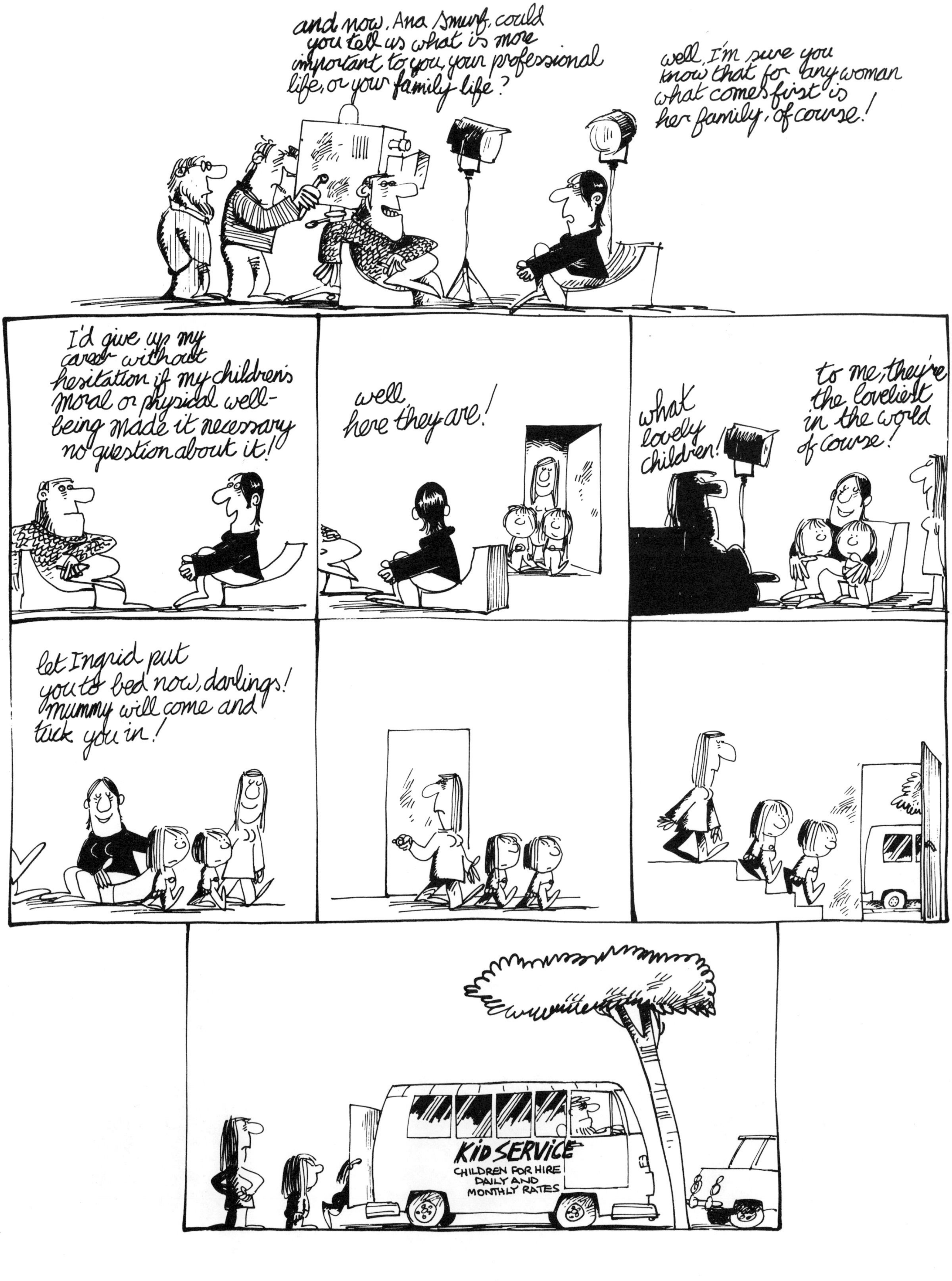
and now, Ana Smurf, could you tell us what is more important to you, your professional life, or your family life?
well, I'm sure you know that for any woman what comes first is her family, of course!
I'd give up my career without hesitation if my children's moral or physical well-being made it necessary no question about it!
well here they are!
what lovely children!
to me, they're the loveliest in the world of course!
let Ingrid put you to bed now, darlings! mummy will come and tuck you in!
KID SERVICE
CHILDREN FOR HIRE
DAILY AND
MONTHLY RATES

our little ones

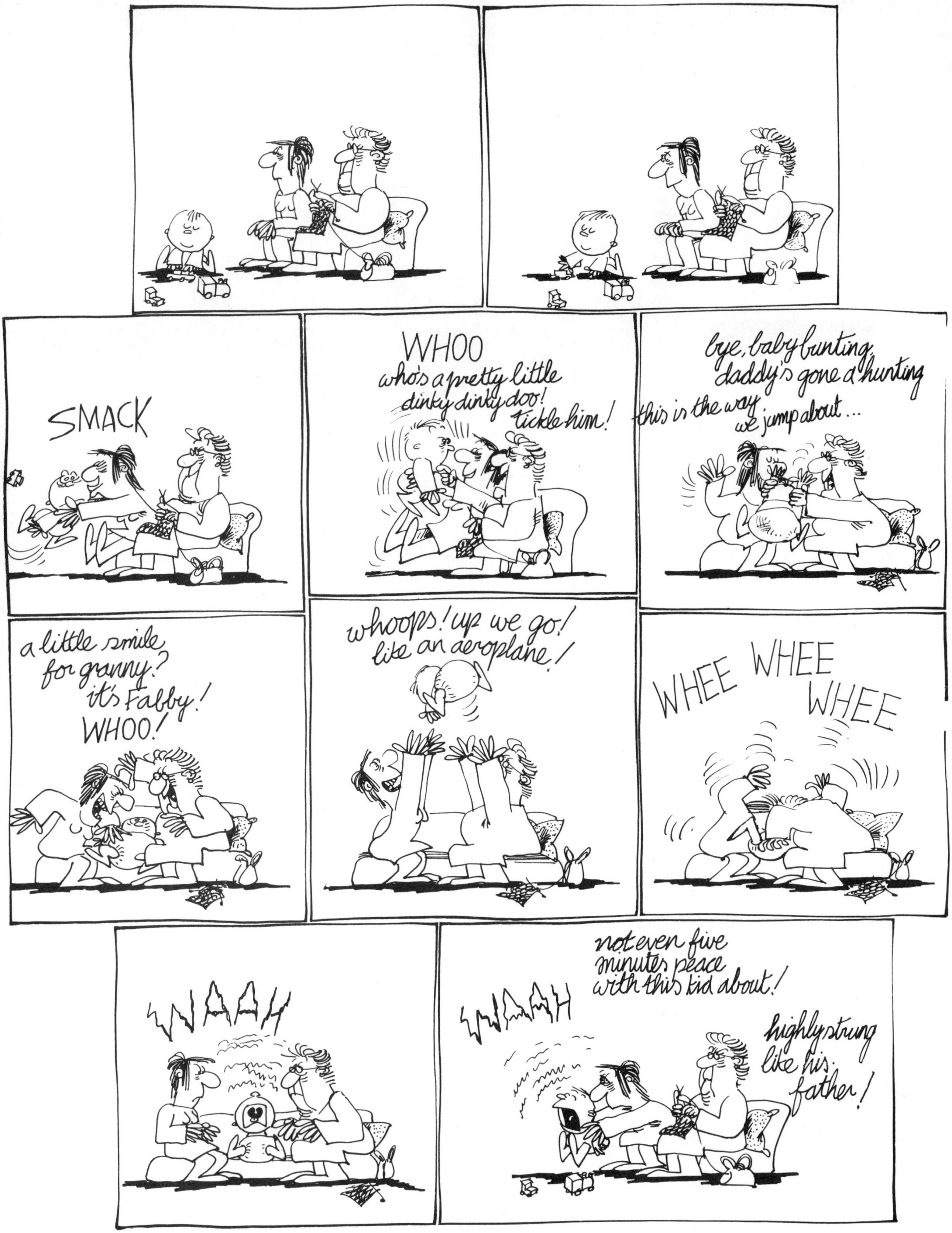
SMACK
WHOO
who's a pretty little dinky dinky doo!
tickle him!
bye, baby bunting, daddy's gone a hunting
this is the way we jump about...
a little smile for granny?
it's Fabby!
WHOO!
whoops! up we go! like an aeroplane!
WHEE WHEE WHEE
WAAAH
WAAAH
not even five minutes peace with this kid about!
highly strung like his father!

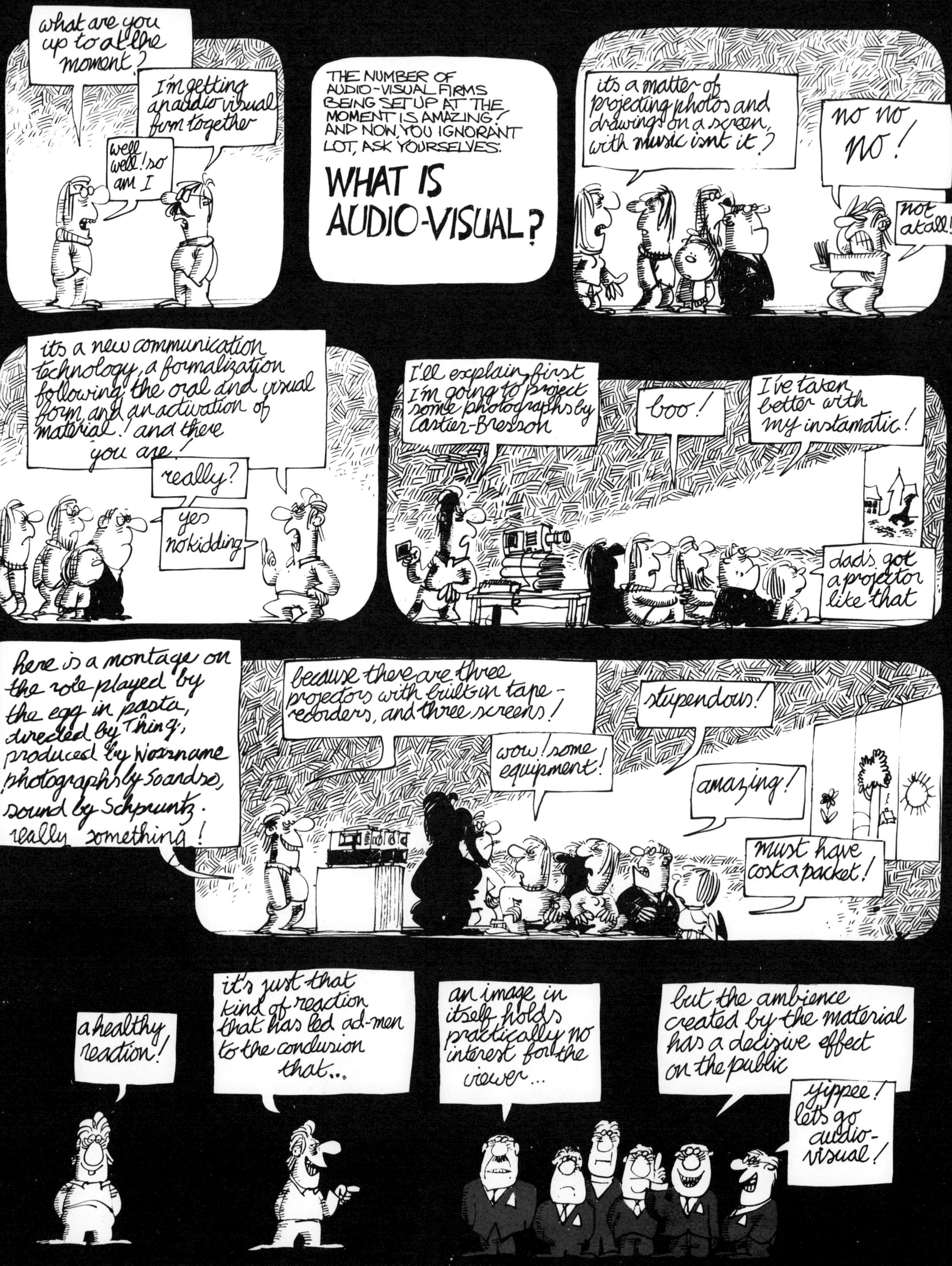
what are you up to at the moment?
I'm getting an audio visual firm together
well well! so am I
THE NUMBER OF AUDIO-VISUAL FIRMS BEING SET UP AT THE MOMENT IS AMAZING! AND NOW, YOU IGNORANT LOT, ASK YOURSELVES:
WHAT IS AUDIO-VISUAL?
its a matter of projecting photos and drawings on a screen, with music isnt it?
no no NO!
not atall!
its a new communication technology, a formalization following the oral and visual form and an activation of material! and there you are!
really?
yes nokidding
I'll explain, first I'm going to project some photographs by Cartier-Bresson
boo!
I've taken better with my instamatic!
dad's got a projector like that
here is a montage on the role played by the egg in pasta, directed by Thing, produced by Wotsname photographs by Soandso, sound by Schpruntz. really something!
because there are three projectors with built-in tape-recorders, and three screens!
stupendous!
wow! some equipment!
amazing!
must have cost a packet!
a healthy reaction!
it's just that kind of reaction that has led ad-men to the conclusion that...
an image in itself holds practically no interest for the viewer...
but the ambience created by the material has a decisive effect on the public
yippee! lets go audio-visual!

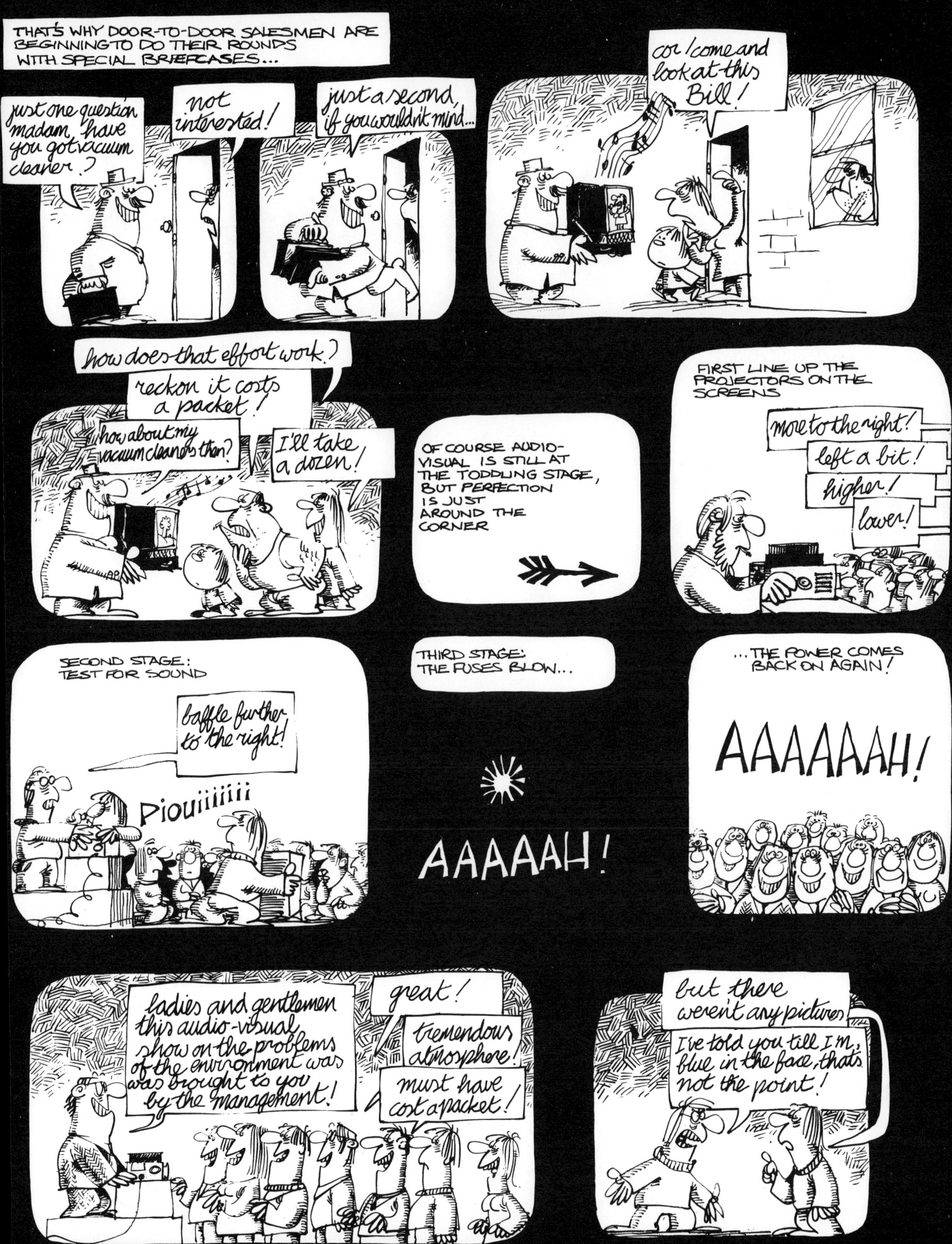
THAT'S WHY DOOR-TO-DOOR SALESMEN ARE BEGINNING TO DO THEIR ROUNDS WITH SPECIAL BRIEFCASES...
just one question madam, have you got vacuum cleaner?
not interested!
just a second, if you wouldn't mind...
cor! come and look at this Bill!
how does that effort work?
reckon it costs a packet!
how about my vacuum cleaners then?
I'll take a dozen!
OF COURSE AUDIO-VISUAL IS STILL AT THE TODDLING STAGE, BUT PERFECTION IS JUST AROUND THE CORNER
FIRST LINE UP THE PROJECTORS ON THE SCREENS
more to the right!
left a bit!
higher!
lower!
SECOND STAGE: TEST FOR SOUND
baffle further to the right!
Piouiiiiiii
THIRD STAGE: THE FUSES BLOW...
AAAAAH!
... THE POWER COMES BACK ON AGAIN!
AAAAAAH!
ladies and gentlemen this audio-visual show on the problems of the environment was was brought to you by the management!
great!
tremendous atmosphere!
must have cost a packet!
but there weren't any pictures
I've told you till I'm blue in the face, that's not the point!

a lily in grape juice

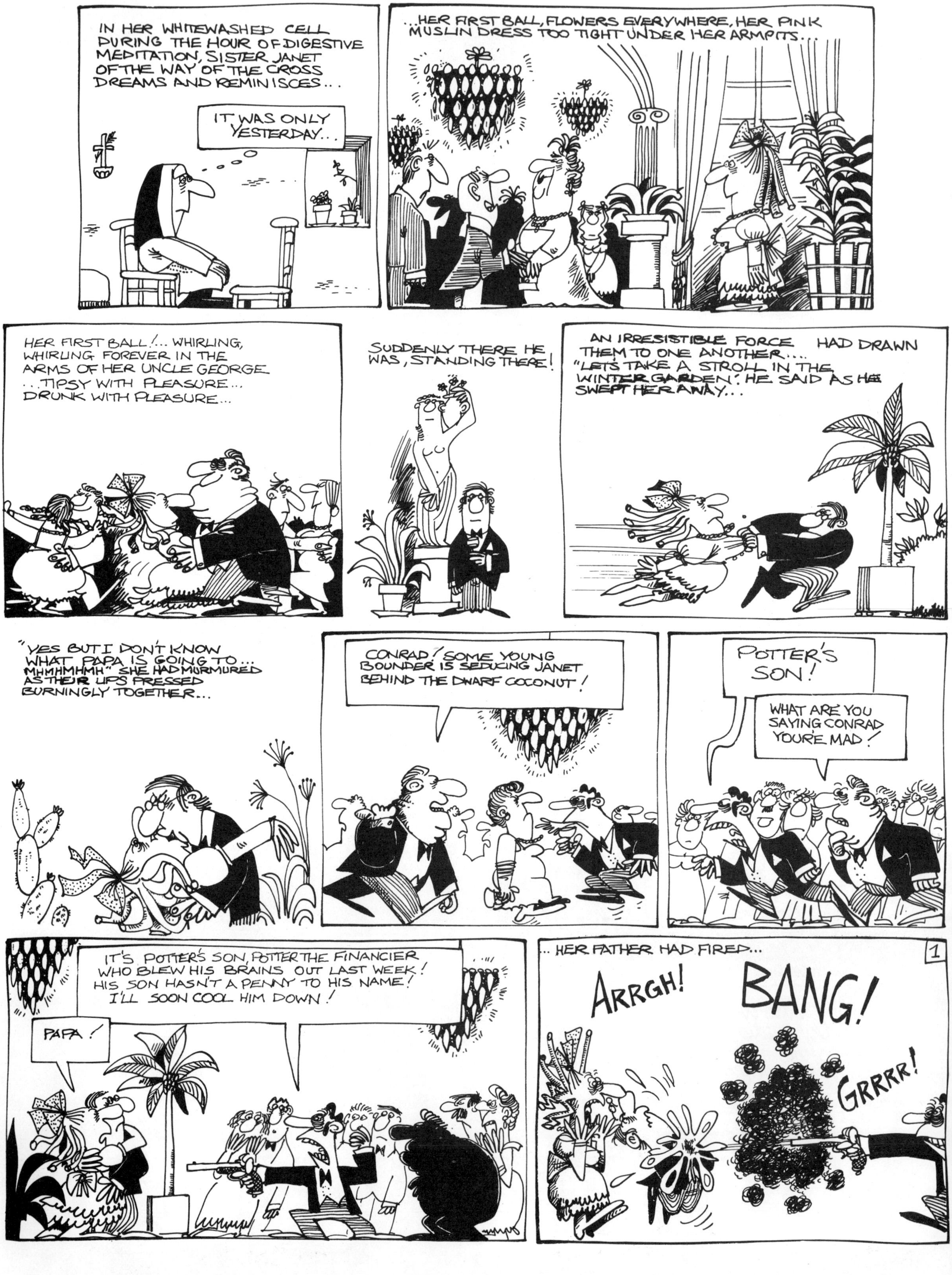

IN HER WHITEWASHED CELL DURING THE HOUR OF DIGESTIVE MEDITATION, SISTER JANET OF THE WAY OF THE CROSS DREAMS AND REMINISCES...
IT WAS ONLY YESTERDAY...
...HER FIRST BALL, FLOWERS EVERYWHERE, HER PINK MUSLIN DRESS TOO TIGHT UNDER HER ARMPITS...
HER FIRST BALL!... WHIRLING, WHIRLING FOREVER IN THE ARMS OF HER UNCLE GEORGE ...TIPSY WITH PLEASURE... DRUNK WITH PLEASURE...
SUDDENLY THERE HE WAS, STANDING THERE!
AN IRRESISTIBLE FORCE HAD DRAWN THEM TO ONE ANOTHER.... "LETS TAKE A STROLL IN THE WINTER GARDEN" HE SAID AS HE SWEPT HER AWAY...
"YES BUT I DON'T KNOW WHAT PAPA IS GOING TO... MHMHMHMH" SHE HAD MURMURED AS THEIR LIPS PRESSED BURNINGLY TOGETHER...
CONRAD! SOME YOUNG BOUNDER IS SEDUCING JANET BEHIND THE DWARF COCONUT!
POTTER'S SON!
WHAT ARE YOU SAYING CONRAD YOU'RE MAD!
IT'S POTTER'S SON, POTTER THE FINANCIER WHO BLEW HIS BRAINS OUT LAST WEEK! HIS SON HASN'T A PENNY TO HIS NAME! I'LL SOON COOL HIM DOWN!
PAPA!
...HER FATHER HAD FIRED...
1
ARRGH!
BANG!
GRRRR!

AND WHILE THEY RUSHED OFF TO GET THE CLEANING LADY, HER FROZEN ARMS HAD HELD THE DYING MAN...

THE YOUNG GIRL NEVER GOT OVER THIS FRIGHTFUL BLOW. WHEN ALL ELSE FAILED, SHE WAS TAKEN ON A PILGRIMAGE TO THE MIRACULOUS STATUE OF SAINT PARKINSON...

..WHICH EVERY YEAR SHEDS TEARS OF BLOOD ON THE VERY DAY THE INCOME TAX DEMAND ARRIVES AT THE BISHOP'S PALACE...

KNEELING BEFORE THE SAINT, JANET FELT THE CALL. EIGHT HOURS 'LATER SHE ENTERED THE AUSTERE ORDER OF THE DESSICATED CAROTIDS...

IN HER CELL TINGED BLUE BY THE COLD SUN OF DAWN, SISTER JANET OF THE WAY OF THE CROSS DREAMS AND REMEMBERS...

IT WAS ONLY YESTERDAY...

FOR MONTHS SHE STROVE TO FORGET HERSELF IN PRAYER AND IN THE HUMBLEST CHORES WHICH, OF COURSE HAVE THEIR OWN NOBILITY...

BUTCHERING A PIG FOR EXAMPLE

BUT ALAS, HER DELICATE HEALTH WAS NOT TO WITHSTAND THIS HARSH LIFE FOR LONG. HAEMORRHAGES FOLLOWED COUGHING FITS...

RAAAAAGH!

ONE DAY THE CONVENT DOCTOR TOLD HER THE TERRIBLE TRUTH:

I'LL HAVE TO WHIP OUT THOSE TONSILS!

HER NERVE CENTRES PERFECTLY ANAESTHETISED BY A NEEDLE IN THE BEND OF THE ARM AND ANOTHER IN THE GUM SISTER JANET SANG PSALM 59 DURING THE OPERATION

IN HER CELL GILDED BY THE SETTING SUN SISTER JANET LOOKS BACK ON HER JOYFUL CONVALESCENCE...

AND THE DAILY VISITS OF THE YOUNG CLEAR-EYED CHAPLAIN, IN WHOM SHE WAS QUICK TO RECOGNISE A KINDRED SPIRIT...

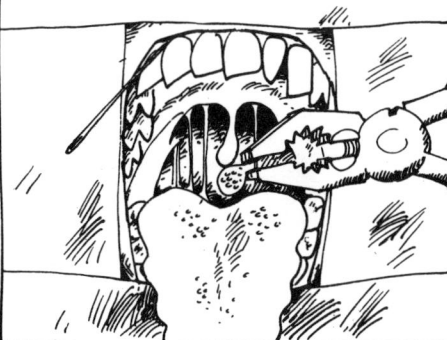

2

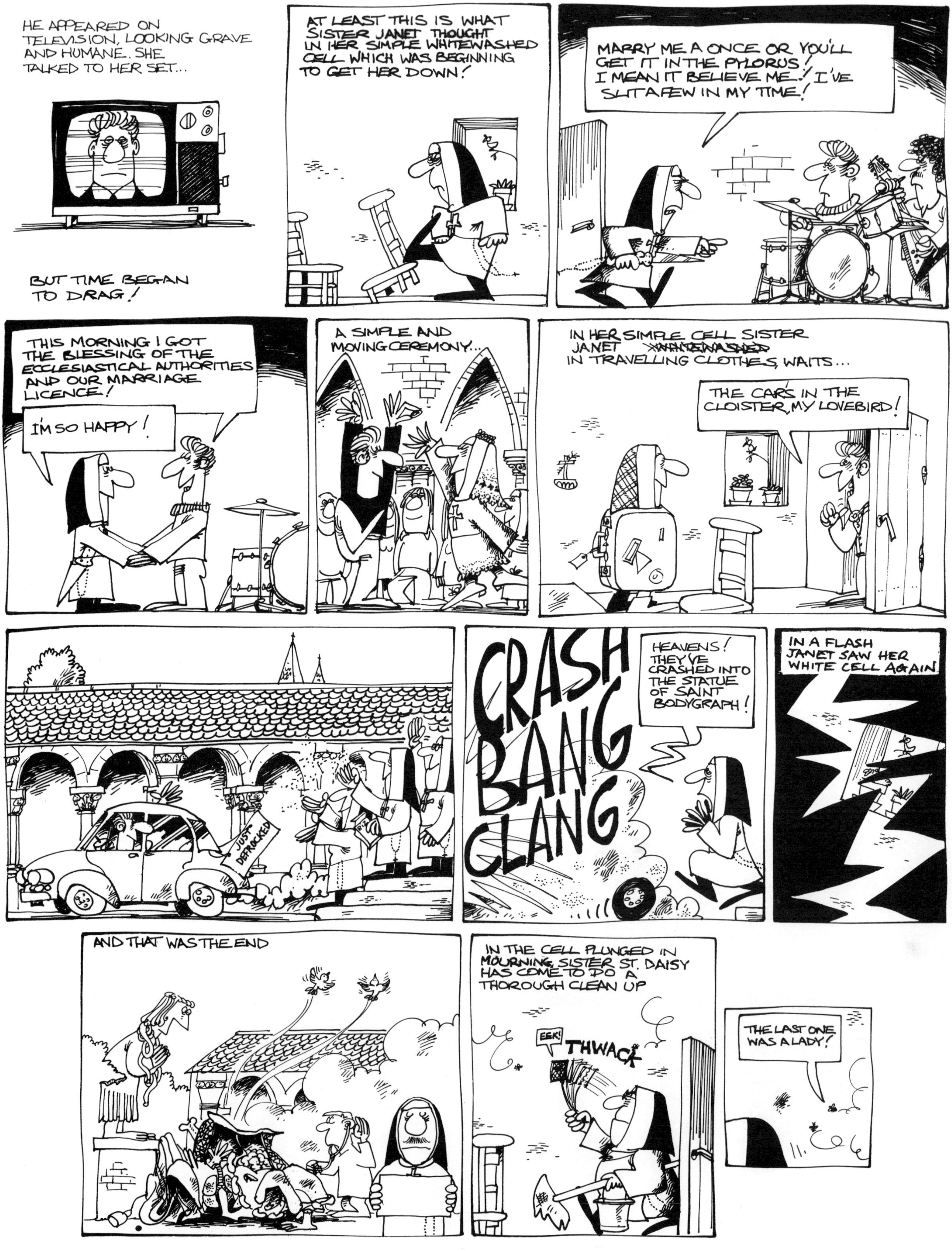

HE APPEARED ON TELEVISION, LOOKING GRAVE AND HUMANE. SHE TALKED TO HER SET...
BUT TIME BEGAN TO DRAG!
AT LEAST THIS IS WHAT SISTER JANET THOUGHT IN HER SIMPLE WHITEWASHED CELL WHICH WAS BEGINNING TO GET HER DOWN!
MARRY ME A ONCE OR YOU'LL GET IT IN THE PYLORUS! I MEAN IT BELIEVE ME! I'VE SLIT A FEW IN MY TIME!
THIS MORNING I GOT THE BLESSING OF THE ECCLESIASTICAL AUTHORITIES AND OUR MARRIAGE LICENCE!
I'M SO HAPPY!
A SIMPLE AND MOVING CEREMONY...
IN HER SIMPLE CELL SISTER JANET WHITEWASHED IN TRAVELLING CLOTHES, WAITS...
THE CAR'S IN THE CLOISTER, MY LOVEBIRD!
JUST DEFROCKED
CRASH
BANG
CLANG
HEAVENS! THEY'VE CRASHED INTO THE STATUE OF SAINT BODYGRAPH!
IN A FLASH JANET SAW HER WHITE CELL AGAIN
AND THAT WAS THE END
IN THE CELL PLUNGED IN MOURNING, SISTER ST. DAISY HAS COME TO DO A THOROUGH CLEAN UP
EEK!
THWACK
THE LAST ONE WAS A LADY!

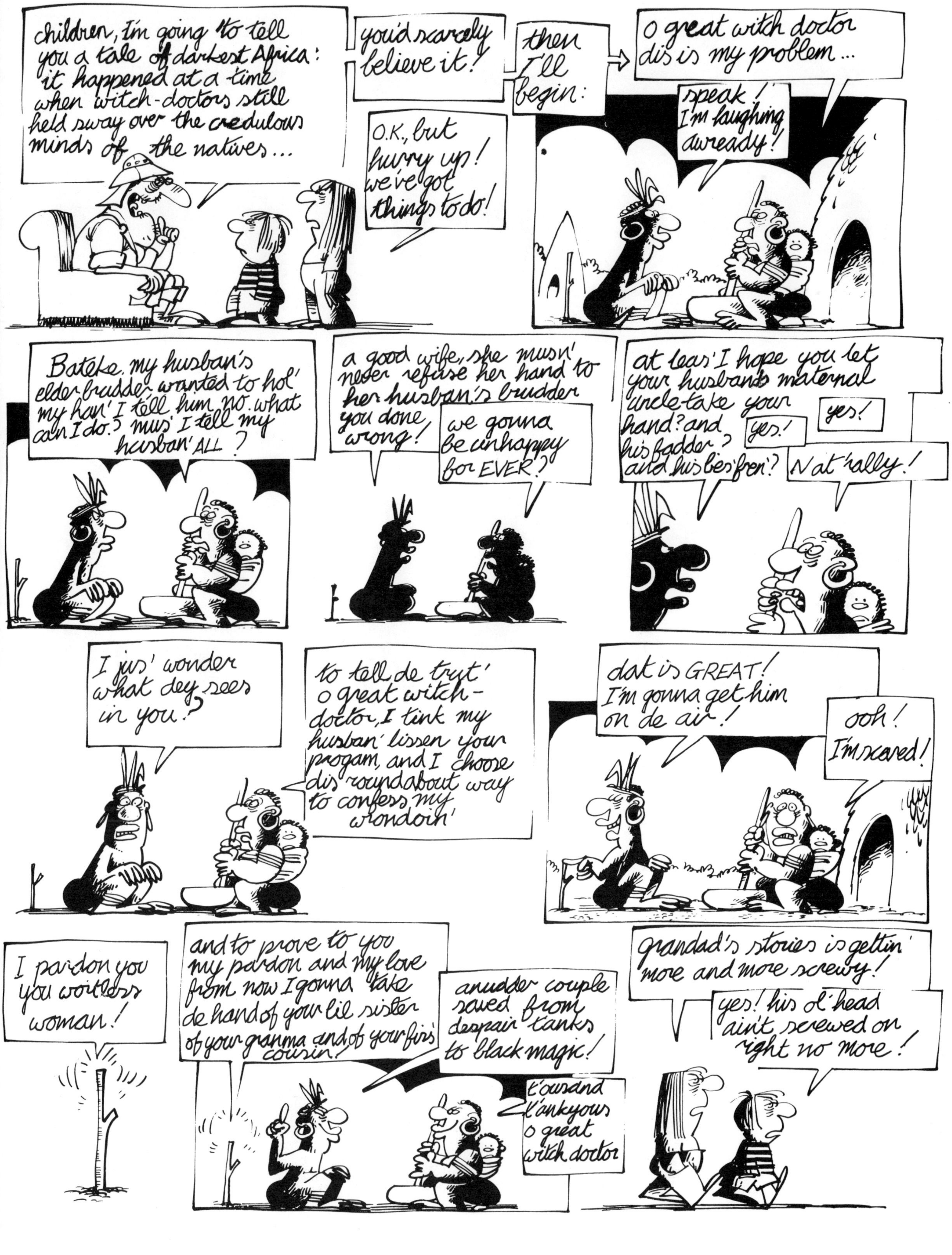
children, I'm going to tell you a tale of darkest Africa: it happened at a time when witch-doctors still held sway over the credulous minds of the natives...
you'd scarcely believe it!
O.K., but hurry up! we've got things to do!
then I'll begin:
o great witch doctor dis is my problem...
speak! I'm laughing awready!
Bateke, my husban's elder brudder wanted to hol' my han' I tell him no. what can I do? mus' I tell my husban' ALL?
a good wife, she musn' never refuse her hand to her husban's brudder you done wrong!
we gonna be unhappy for EVER?
at leas' I hope you let your husban's maternal uncle take your hand? and his fadder? and his bes' fren'?
yes!
yes!
Nat'rally!
I jus' wonder what dey sees in you?
to tell de trut' o great witch-doctor, I tink my husban' lissen your progam, and I choose dis roundabout way to confess my wrondoin'
dat is GREAT! I'm gonna get him on de air!
ooh! I'm scared!
I pardon you you worthless woman!
and to prove to you my pardon and my love from now I gonna take de hand of your lil sister of your granma and of your firs' cousin!
anudder couple saved from despair tanks to black magic!
t'ousand t'ankyous o great witch doctor
grandad's stories is gettin' more and more screwy!
yes! his ol' head ain't screwed on right no more!

words

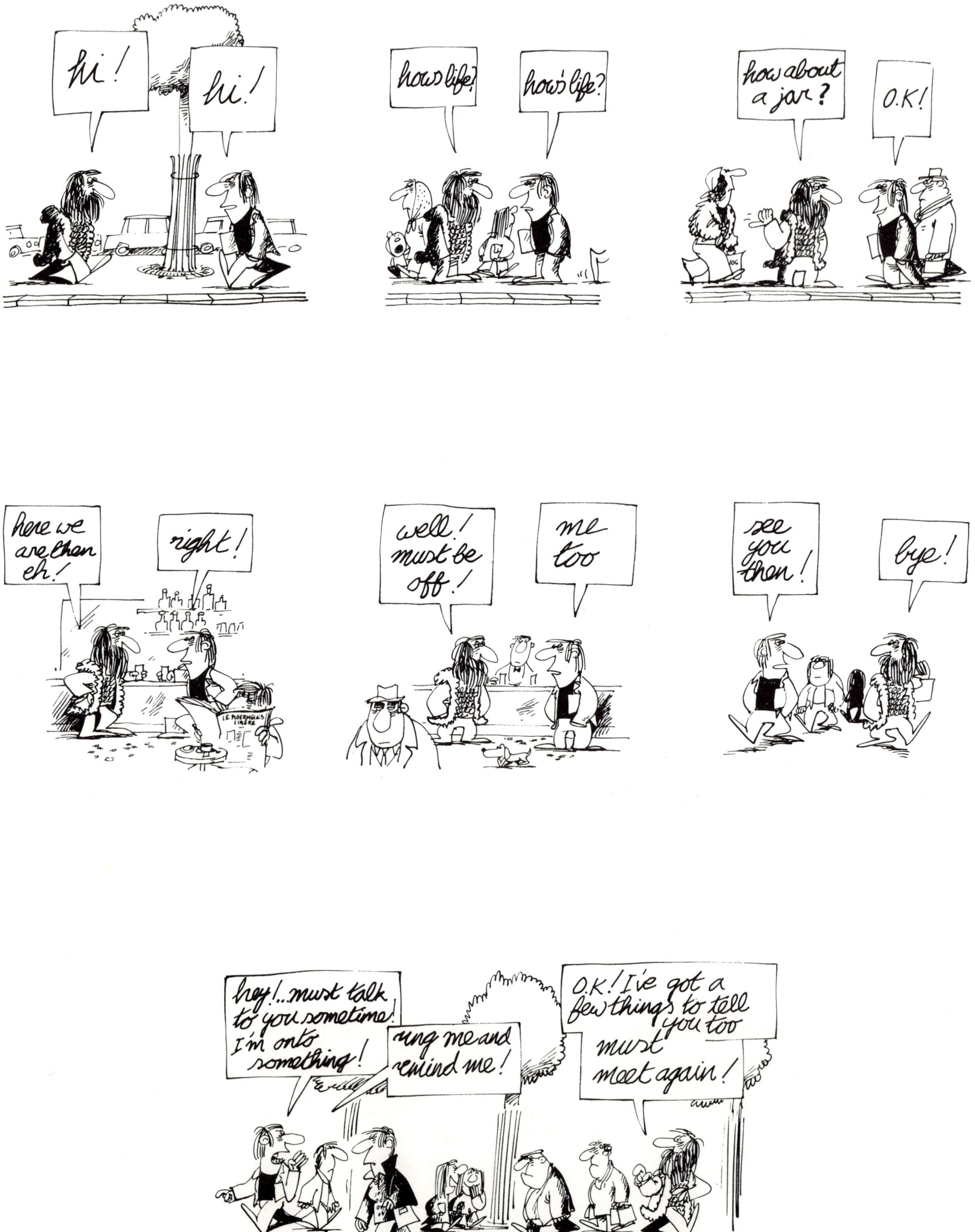
hi!
hi!
hows life?
how's life?
how about a jar?
O.K!
here we are then eh!
right!
well! must be off!
me too
see you then!
bye!
hey!...must talk to you sometime! I'm onto something!
ring me and remind me!
O.K! I've got a few things to tell you too must meet again!

frustration page

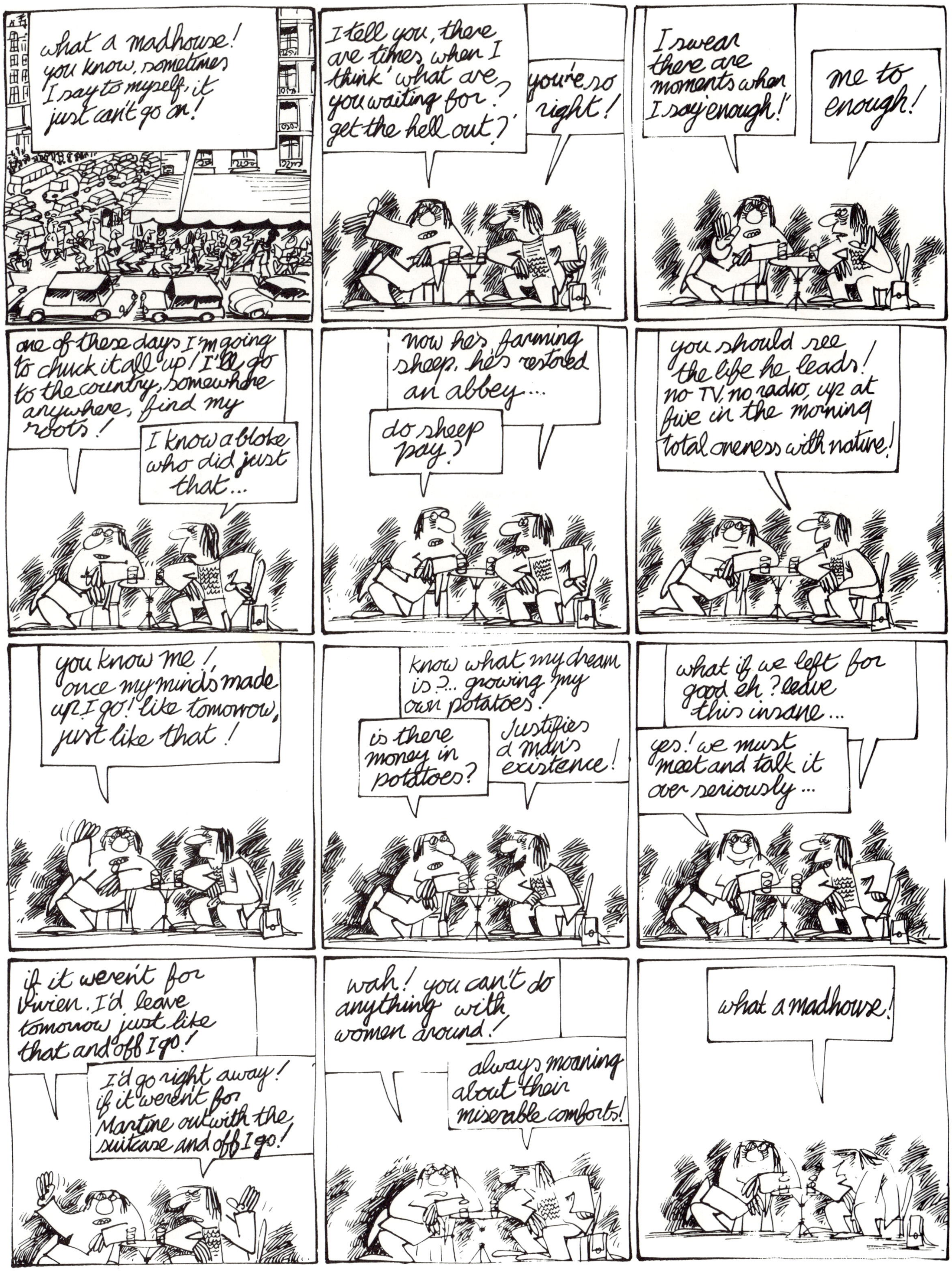
what a madhouse! you know, sometimes I say to myself, it just can't go on!
I tell you, there are times when I think 'what are you waiting for? get the hell out?'
you're so right!
I swear there are moments when I say 'enough!'
me too enough!
one of these days I'm going to chuck it all up! I'll go to the country, somewhere anywhere, find my roots!
I know a bloke who did just that...
now he's farming sheep, he's restored an abbey...
do sheep pay?
you should see the life he leads! no TV, no radio, up at five in the morning total oneness with nature!
you know me! once my mind's made up I go! like tomorrow, just like that!
know what my dream is?... growing my own potatoes!
is there money in potatoes?
justifies a man's existence!
what if we left for good eh? leave this insane...
yes! we must meet and talk it over seriously...
if it weren't for Vivien, I'd leave tomorrow just like that and off I go!
I'd go right away! if it weren't for Martine out with the suitcase and off I go!
wah! you can't do anything with women around!
always moaning about their miserable comforts!
what a madhouse!

an evening at home

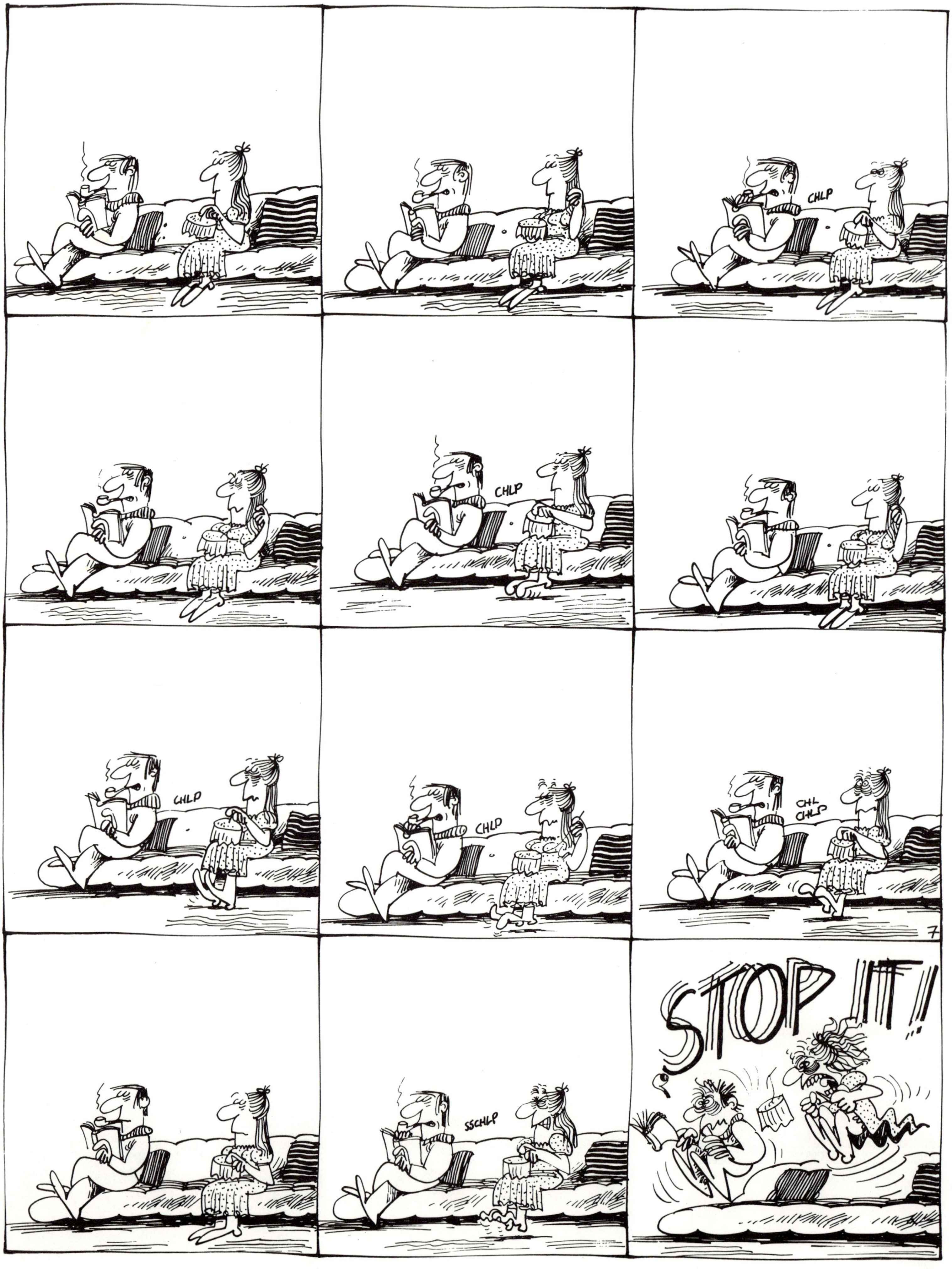
CHLP
CHLP
CHLP
CHLP
CHL
CHLP
SSCHLP
STOP IT!!

lust for life

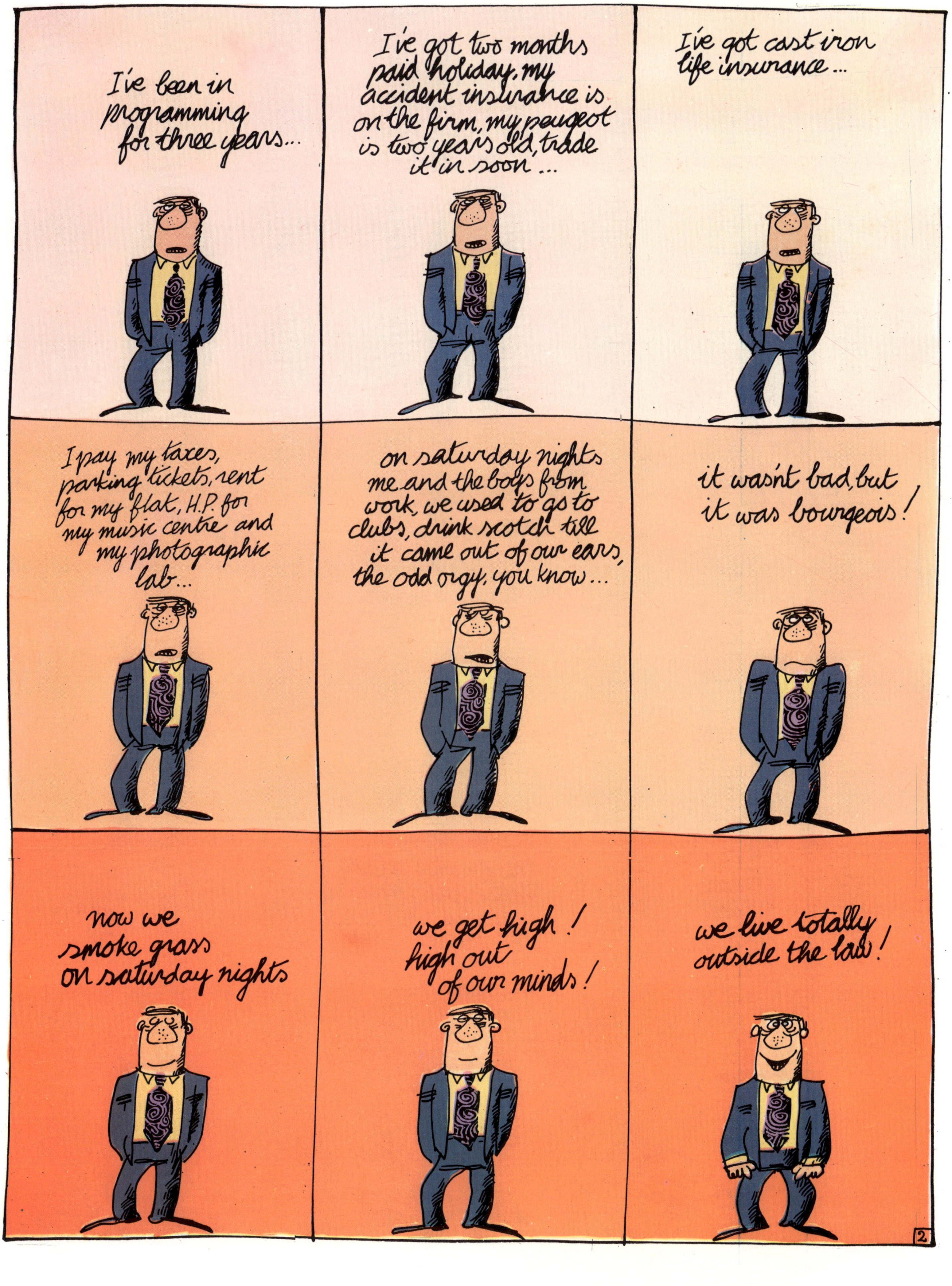

I've been in programming for three years...
I've got two months paid holiday, my accident insurance is on the firm, my peugeot is two years old, trade it in soon...
I've got cast iron life insurance...
I pay my taxes, parking tickets, rent for my flat, H.P. for my music centre and my photographic lab...
on saturday nights me and the boys from work, we used to go to clubs, drink scotch till it came out of our ears, the odd orgy, you know...
it wasn't bad, but it was bourgeois!
now we smoke grass on saturday nights
we get high! high out of our minds!
we live totally outside the law!
2

nearer my god to thee

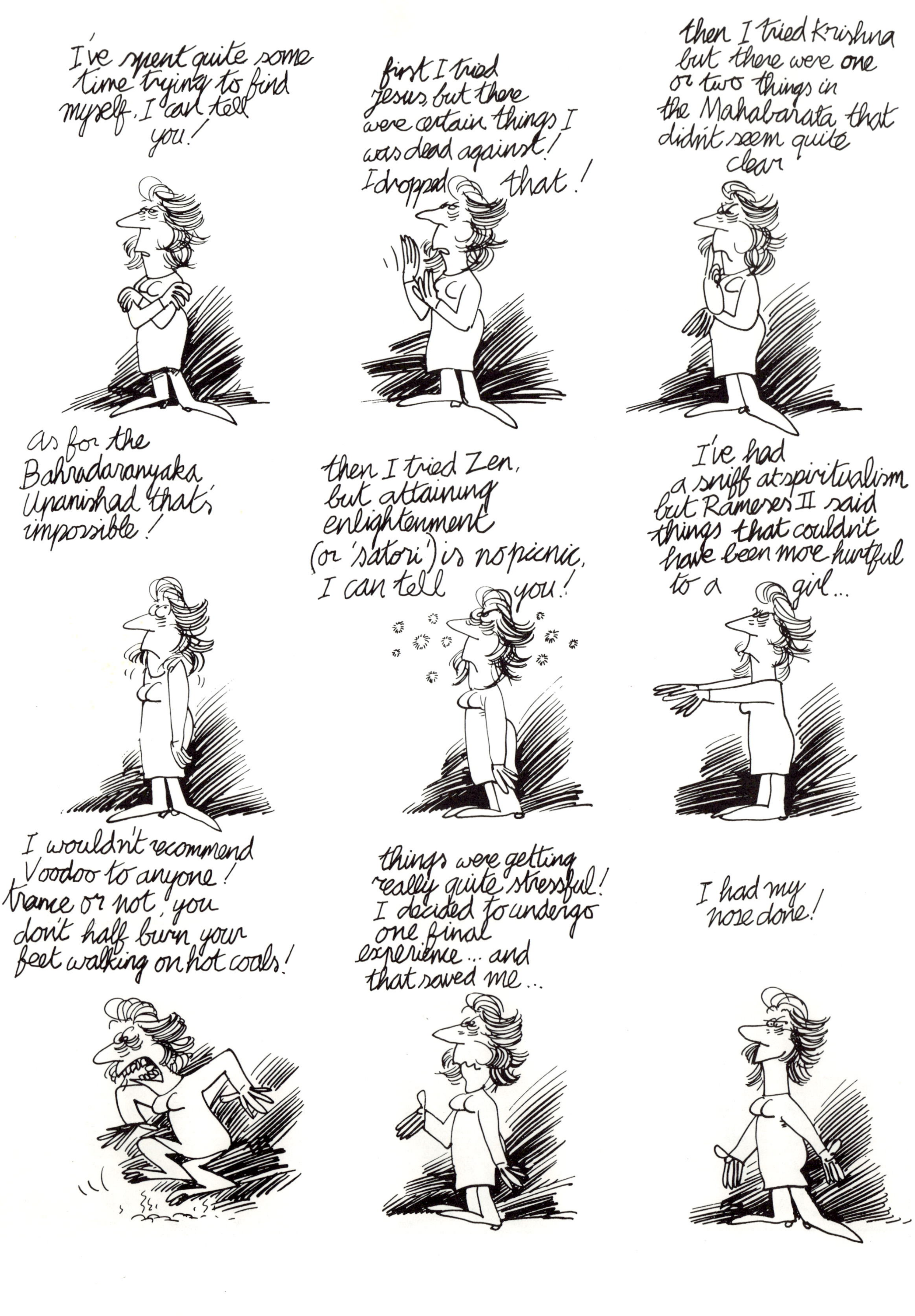
I've spent quite some time trying to find myself, I can tell you!
first I tried Jesus, but there were certain things I was dead against! I dropped that!
then I tried Krishna but there were one or two things in the Mahabarata that didn't seem quite clear
as for the Bahradaranyaka Upanishad that's impossible!
then I tried Zen, but attaining enlightenment (or 'satori') is no picnic, I can tell you!
I've had a sniff at spiritualism but Rameses II said things that couldn't have been more hurtful to a girl...
I wouldn't recommend Voodoo to anyone! trance or not, you don't half burn your feet walking on hot coals!
things were getting really quite stressful! I decided to undergo one final experience... and that saved me...
I had my nose done!

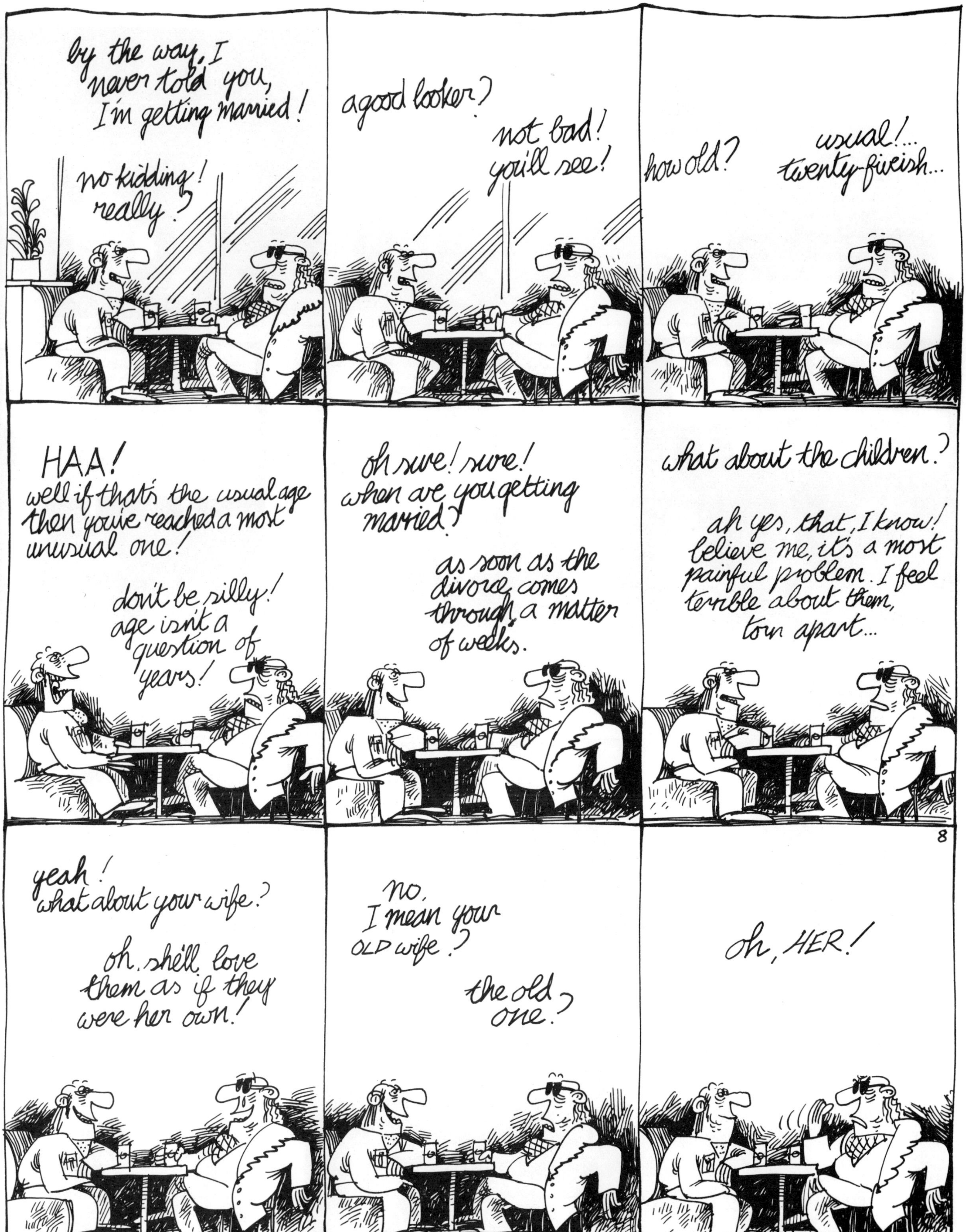
by the way, I never told you, I'm getting married!
no kidding! really?
a good looker?
not bad! you'll see!
how old?
usual!... twenty-fiveish...
HAA! well if that's the usual age then you've reached a most unusual one!
don't be silly! age isn't a question of years!
oh sure! sure! when are you getting married?
as soon as the divorce comes through, a matter of weeks.
what about the children?
ah yes, that, I know! believe me, it's a most painful problem. I feel terrible about them, torn apart...
yeah! what about your wife?
oh, she'll love them as if they were her own!
no, I mean your OLD wife?
the old one?
oh, HER!

school of tension

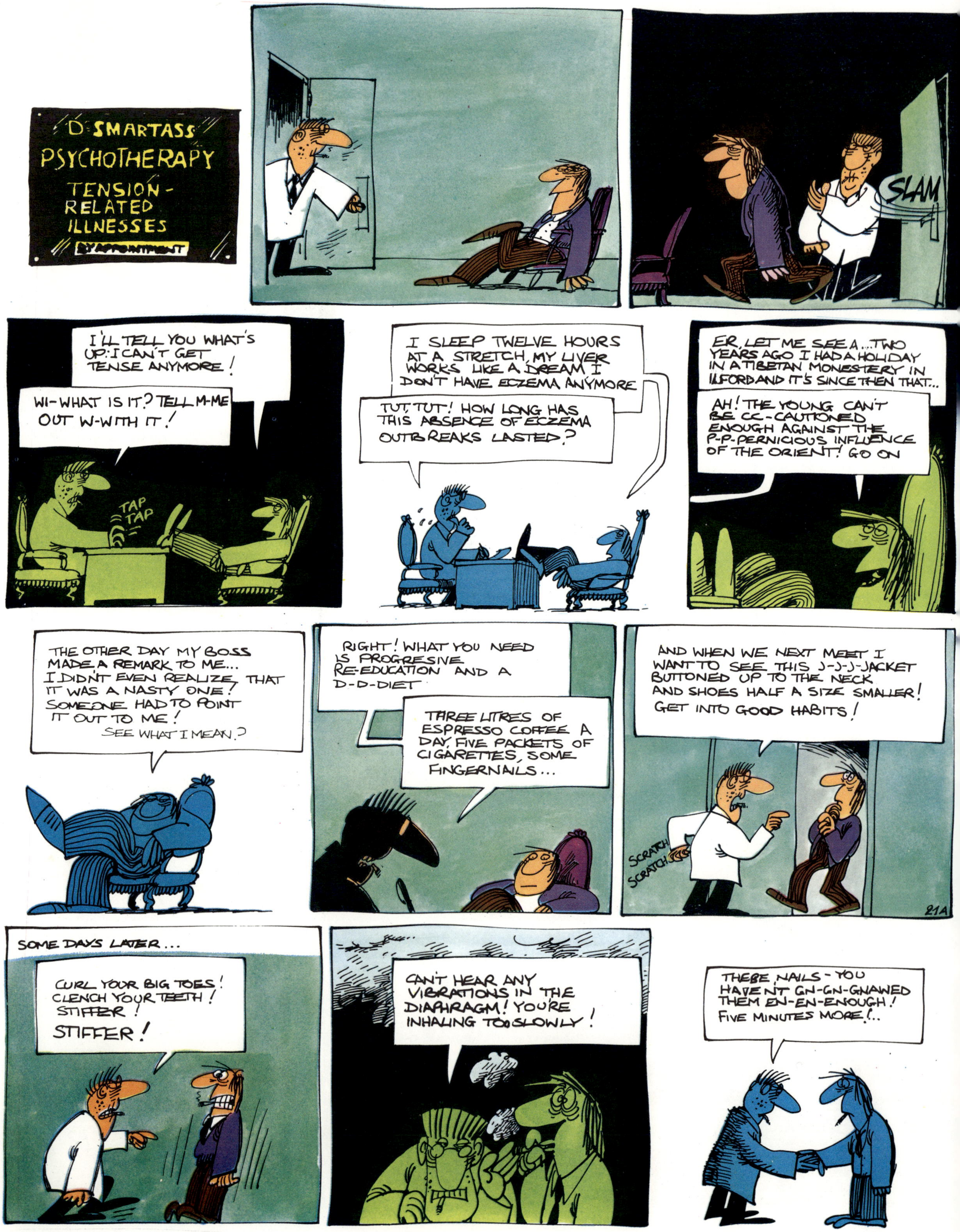

D. SMARTASS
PSYCHOTHERAPY
TENSION-RELATED ILLNESSES
BY APPOINTMENT
SLAM
I'LL TELL YOU WHAT'S UP: I CAN'T GET TENSE ANYMORE!
WI-WHAT IS IT? TELL M-ME OUT W-WITH IT!
TAP TAP
I SLEEP TWELVE HOURS AT A STRETCH, MY LIVER WORKS LIKE A DREAM I DON'T HAVE ECZEMA ANYMORE
TUT, TUT! HOW LONG HAS THIS ABSENCE OF ECZEMA OUTBREAKS LASTED?
ER, LET ME SEE A... TWO YEARS AGO I HAD A HOLIDAY IN A TIBETAN MONESTERY IN ILFORD AND IT'S SINCE THEN THAT...
AH! THE YOUNG CAN'T BE CC-CAUTIONED ENOUGH AGAINST THE P-P-PERNICIOUS INFLUENCE OF THE ORIENT! GO ON
THE OTHER DAY MY BOSS MADE A REMARK TO ME... I DIDN'T EVEN REALIZE THAT IT WAS A NASTY ONE! SOMEONE HAD TO POINT IT OUT TO ME! SEE WHAT I MEAN?
RIGHT! WHAT YOU NEED IS PROGRESIVE RE-EDUCATION AND A D-D-DIET
THREE LITRES OF ESPRESSO COFFEE A DAY, FIVE PACKETS OF CIGARETTES, SOME FINGERNAILS...
AND WHEN WE NEXT MEET I WANT TO SEE THIS J-J-J-JACKET BUTTONED UP TO THE NECK AND SHOES HALF A SIZE SMALLER! GET INTO GOOD HABITS!
SCRATCH SCRATCH
21A
SOME DAYS LATER...
CURL YOUR BIG TOES! CLENCH YOUR TEETH! STIFFER! STIFFER!
CAN'T HEAR ANY VIBRATIONS IN THE DIAPHRAGM! YOU'RE INHALING TOO SLOWLY!
THESE NAILS - YOU HAVEN'T GN-GN-GNAWED THEM EN-EN-ENOUGH! FIVE MINUTES MORE!...

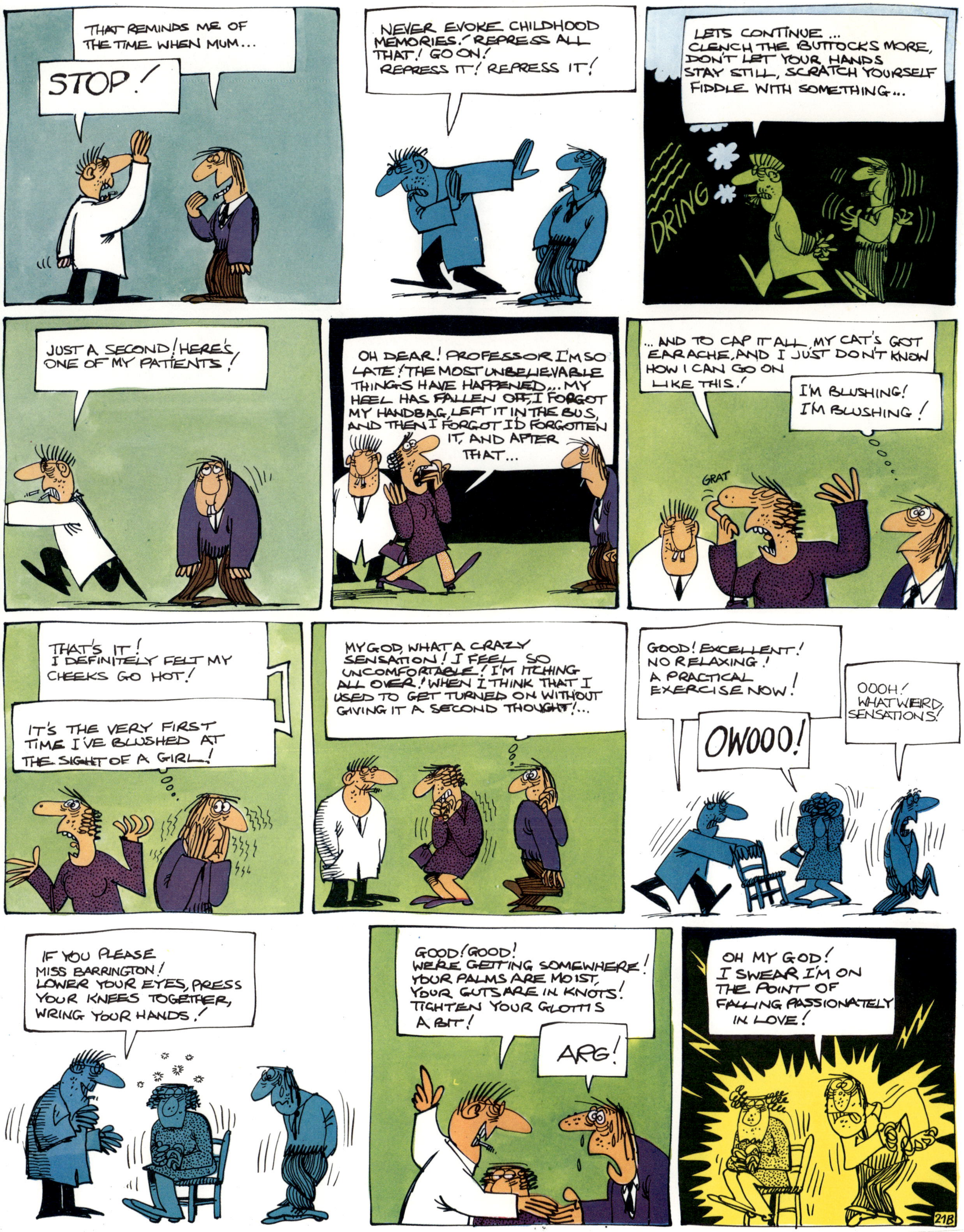
THAT REMINDS ME OF THE TIME WHEN MUM...
STOP!
NEVER EVOKE CHILDHOOD MEMORIES! REPRESS ALL THAT! GO ON! REPRESS IT! REPRESS IT!
LETS CONTINUE... CLENCH THE BUTTOCKS MORE, DON'T LET YOUR HANDS STAY STILL, SCRATCH YOURSELF FIDDLE WITH SOMETHING...
DRING
JUST A SECOND! HERE'S ONE OF MY PATIENTS!
OH DEAR! PROFESSOR I'M SO LATE! THE MOST UNBELIEVABLE THINGS HAVE HAPPENED... MY HEEL HAS FALLEN OFF, I FORGOT MY HANDBAG, LEFT IT IN THE BUS, AND THEN I FORGOT I'D FORGOTTEN IT, AND AFTER THAT...
...AND TO CAP IT ALL MY CAT'S GOT EARACHE, AND I JUST DON'T KNOW HOW I CAN GO ON LIKE THIS!
I'M BLUSHING! I'M BLUSHING!
GRAT
THAT'S IT! I DEFINITELY FELT MY CHEEKS GO HOT!
IT'S THE VERY FIRST TIME I'VE BLUSHED AT THE SIGHT OF A GIRL!
MY GOD, WHAT A CRAZY SENSATION! I FEEL SO UNCOMFORTABLE! I'M ITCHING ALL OVER! WHEN I THINK THAT I USED TO GET TURNED ON WITHOUT GIVING IT A SECOND THOUGHT!...
GOOD! EXCELLENT! NO RELAXING! A PRACTICAL EXERCISE NOW!
OWOOO!
OOOH! WHAT WEIRD SENSATIONS!
IF YOU PLEASE MISS BARRINGTON! LOWER YOUR EYES, PRESS YOUR KNEES TOGETHER, WRING YOUR HANDS!
GOOD! GOOD! WE'RE GETTING SOMEWHERE! YOUR PALMS ARE MOIST, YOUR GUTS ARE IN KNOTS! TIGHTEN YOUR GLOTTIS A BIT!
ARG!
OH MY GOD! I SWEAR I'M ON THE POINT OF FALLING PASSIONATELY IN LOVE!
21B

a familiar tune

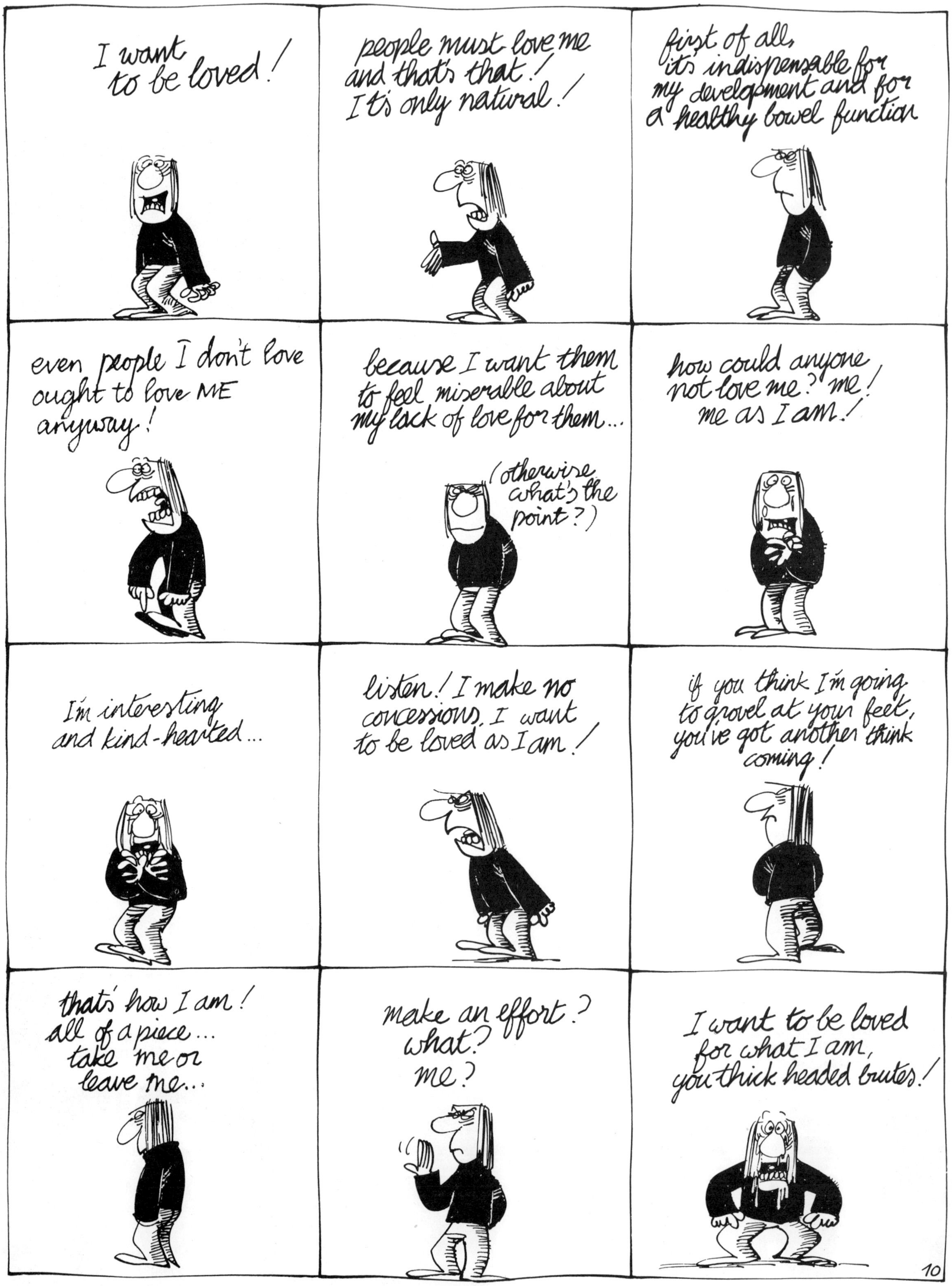
I want to be loved!
people must love me and that's that! It's only natural!
first of all, it's indispensable for my development and for a healthy bowel function
even people I don't love ought to love ME anyway!
because I want them to feel miserable about my lack of love for them...
(otherwise what's the point?)
how could anyone not love me? me! me as I am!
I'm interesting and kind-hearted...
listen! I make no concessions. I want to be loved as I am!
if you think I'm going to grovel at your feet, you've got another think coming!
that's how I am! all of a piece... take me or leave me...
make an effort? what? me?
I want to be loved for what I am, you thick headed brutes!
10

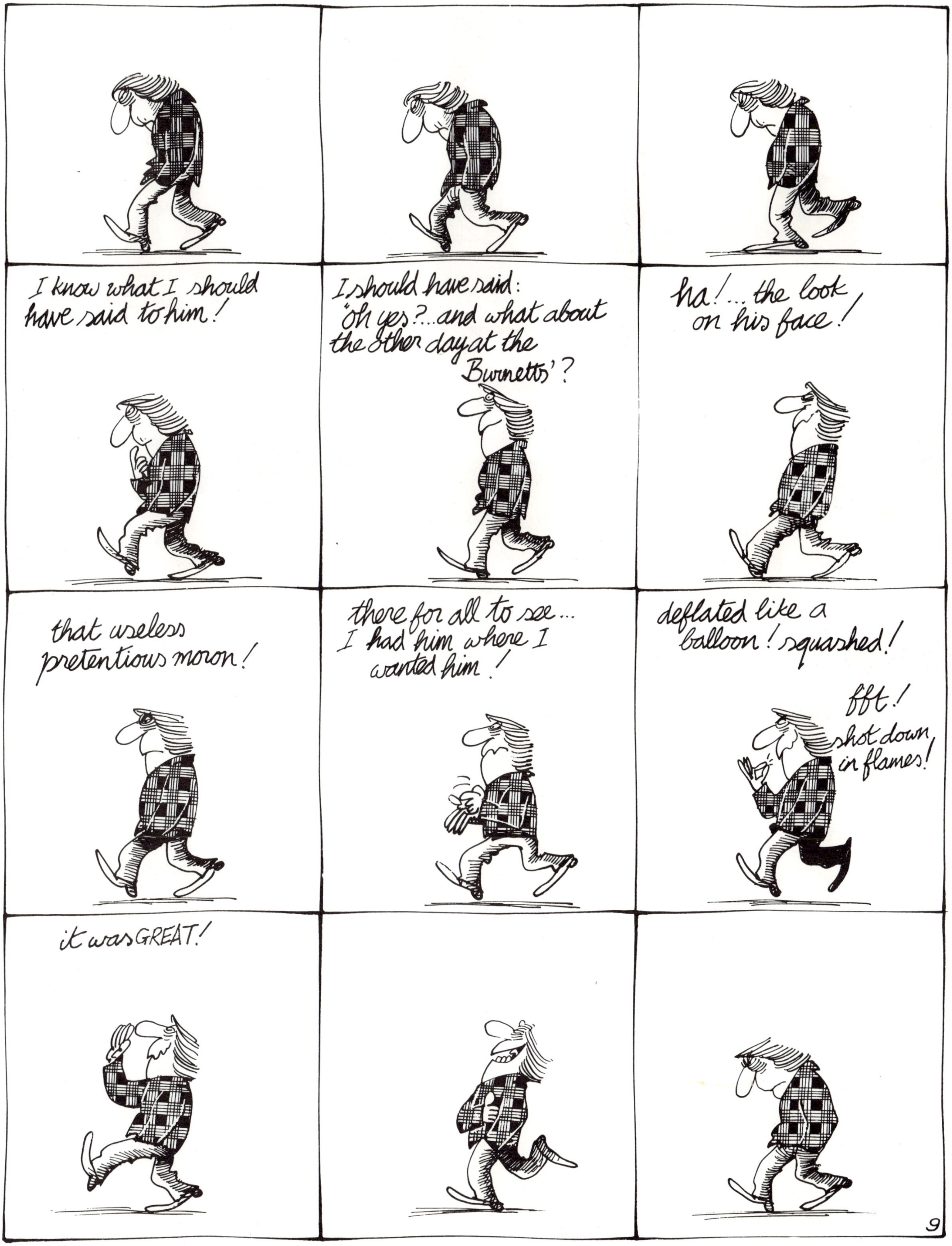
I know what I should have said to him!
I should have said: "oh yes?...and what about the other day at the Burnetts'?
ha!... the look on his face!
that useless pretentious moron!
there for all to see... I had him where I wanted him!
deflated like a balloon! squashed!
fft! shot down in flames!
it was GREAT!

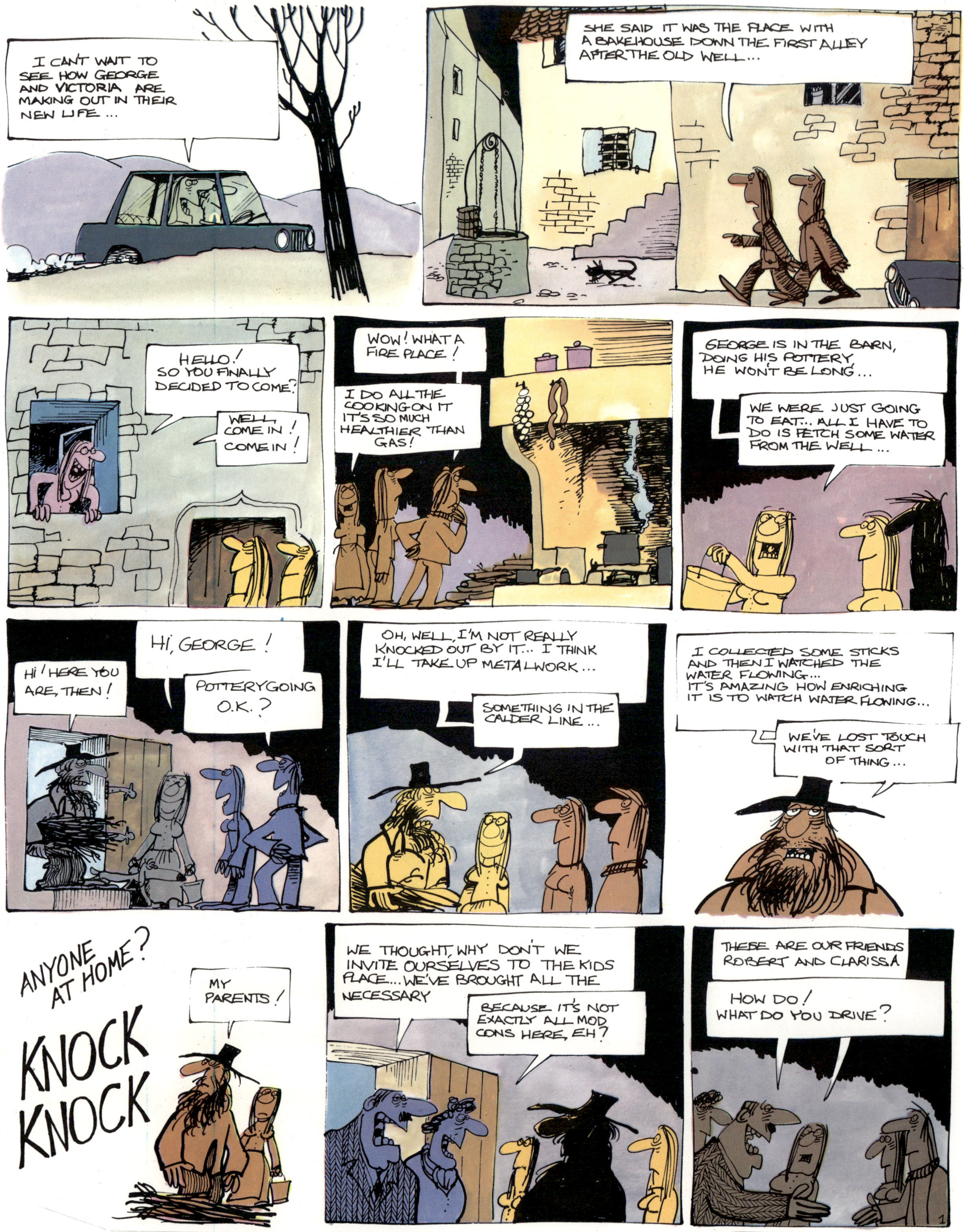

I CAN'T WAIT TO SEE HOW GEORGE AND VICTORIA ARE MAKING OUT IN THEIR NEW LIFE ...
SHE SAID IT WAS THE PLACE WITH A BAKEHOUSE DOWN THE FIRST ALLEY AFTER THE OLD WELL ...
HELLO! SO YOU FINALLY DECIDED TO COME?
WELL, COME IN! COME IN!
WOW! WHAT A FIRE PLACE!
I DO ALL THE COOKING ON IT IT'S SO MUCH HEALTHIER THAN GAS!
GEORGE IS IN THE BARN, DOING HIS POTTERY, HE WON'T BE LONG ...
WE WERE JUST GOING TO EAT... ALL I HAVE TO DO IS FETCH SOME WATER FROM THE WELL ...
HI! HERE YOU ARE, THEN!
HI, GEORGE!
POTTERY GOING O.K.?
OH, WELL, I'M NOT REALLY KNOCKED OUT BY IT... I THINK I'LL TAKE UP METALWORK ...
SOMETHING IN THE CALDER LINE ...
I COLLECTED SOME STICKS AND THEN I WATCHED THE WATER FLOWING... IT'S AMAZING HOW ENRICHING IT IS TO WATCH WATER FLOWING ...
WE'VE LOST TOUCH WITH THAT SORT OF THING ...
ANYONE AT HOME?
KNOCK KNOCK
MY PARENTS!
WE THOUGHT, WHY DON'T WE INVITE OURSELVES TO THE KIDS PLACE... WE'VE BROUGHT ALL THE NECESSARY
BECAUSE IT'S NOT EXACTLY ALL MOD CONS HERE, EH?
THESE ARE OUR FRIENDS ROBERT AND CLARISSA
HOW DO! WHAT DO YOU DRIVE?
1

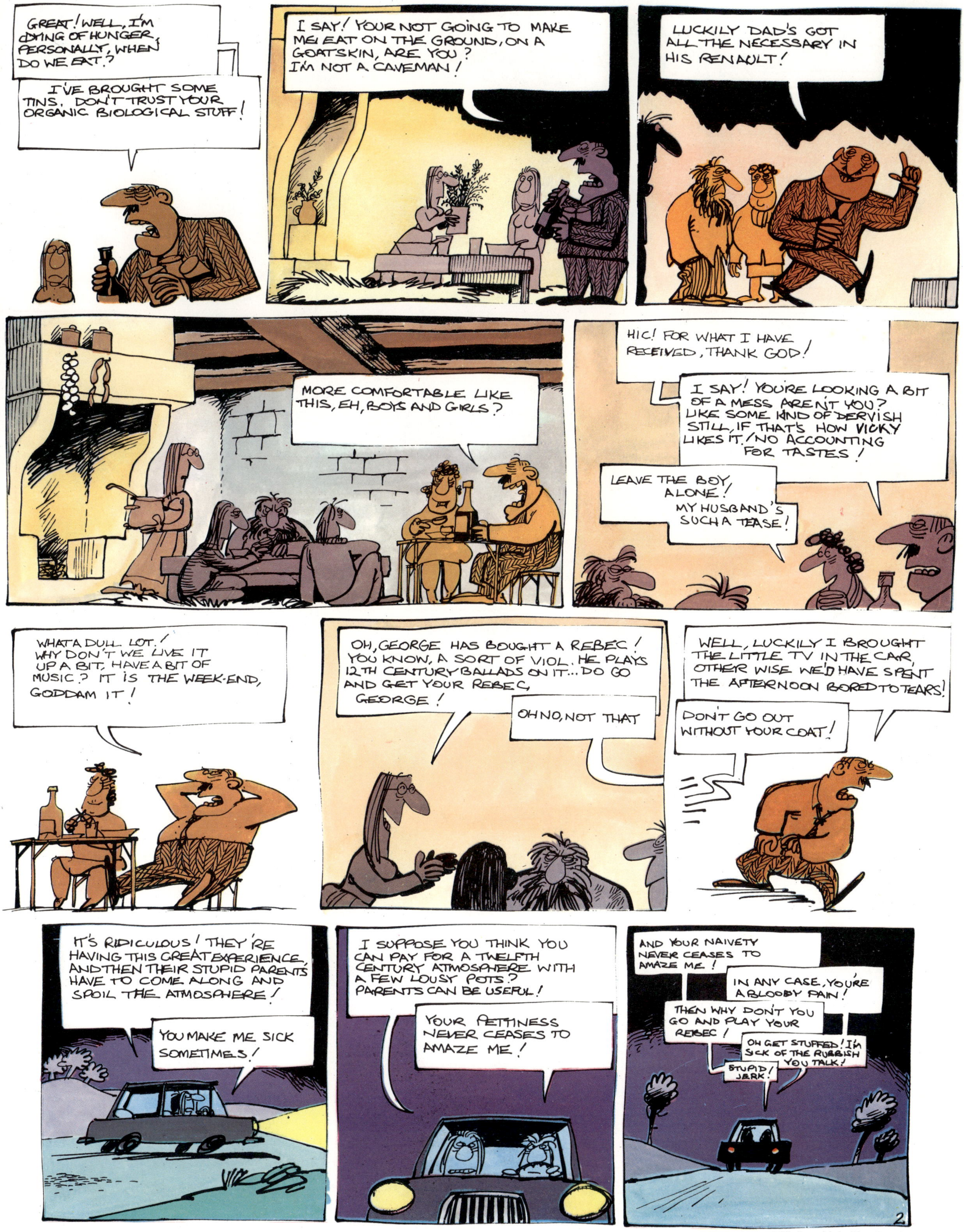
GREAT! WELL, I'M DYING OF HUNGER, PERSONALLY, WHEN DO WE EAT?
I'VE BROUGHT SOME TINS. DON'T TRUST YOUR ORGANIC BIOLOGICAL STUFF!
I SAY! YOUR NOT GOING TO MAKE ME EAT ON THE GROUND, ON A GOATSKIN, ARE YOU? I'M NOT A CAVEMAN!
LUCKILY DAD'S GOT ALL THE NECESSARY IN HIS RENAULT!
MORE COMFORTABLE LIKE THIS, EH, BOYS AND GIRLS?
HIC! FOR WHAT I HAVE RECEIVED, THANK GOD!
I SAY! YOU'RE LOOKING A BIT OF A MESS AREN'T YOU? LIKE SOME KIND OF DERVISH STILL, IF THAT'S HOW VICKY LIKES IT. NO ACCOUNTING FOR TASTES!
LEAVE THE BOY ALONE! MY HUSBAND'S SUCH A TEASE!
WHAT A DULL LOT! WHY DON'T WE LIVE IT UP A BIT, HAVE A BIT OF MUSIC? IT IS THE WEEK-END, GODDAM IT!
OH, GEORGE HAS BOUGHT A REBEC! YOU KNOW, A SORT OF VIOL. HE PLAYS 12TH CENTURY BALLADS ON IT... DO GO AND GET YOUR REBEC, GEORGE!
OH NO, NOT THAT
WELL, LUCKILY I BROUGHT THE LITTLE TV IN THE CAR, OTHERWISE WE'D HAVE SPENT THE AFTERNOON BORED TO TEARS!
DON'T GO OUT WITHOUT YOUR COAT!
IT'S RIDICULOUS! THEY'RE HAVING THIS GREAT EXPERIENCE, AND THEN THEIR STUPID PARENTS HAVE TO COME ALONG AND SPOIL THE ATMOSPHERE!
YOU MAKE ME SICK SOMETIMES!
I SUPPOSE YOU THINK YOU CAN PAY FOR A TWELFTH CENTURY ATMOSPHERE WITH A FEW LOUSY POTS? PARENTS CAN BE USEFUL!
YOUR PETTINESS NEVER CEASES TO AMAZE ME!
AND YOUR NAIVETY NEVER CEASES TO AMAZE ME!
IN ANY CASE, YOU'RE A BLOODY PAIN!
THEN WHY DON'T YOU GO AND PLAY YOUR REBEC!
OH GET STUFFED! I'M SICK OF THE RUBBISH YOU TALK!
STUPID JERK!
2

ode to Eugene

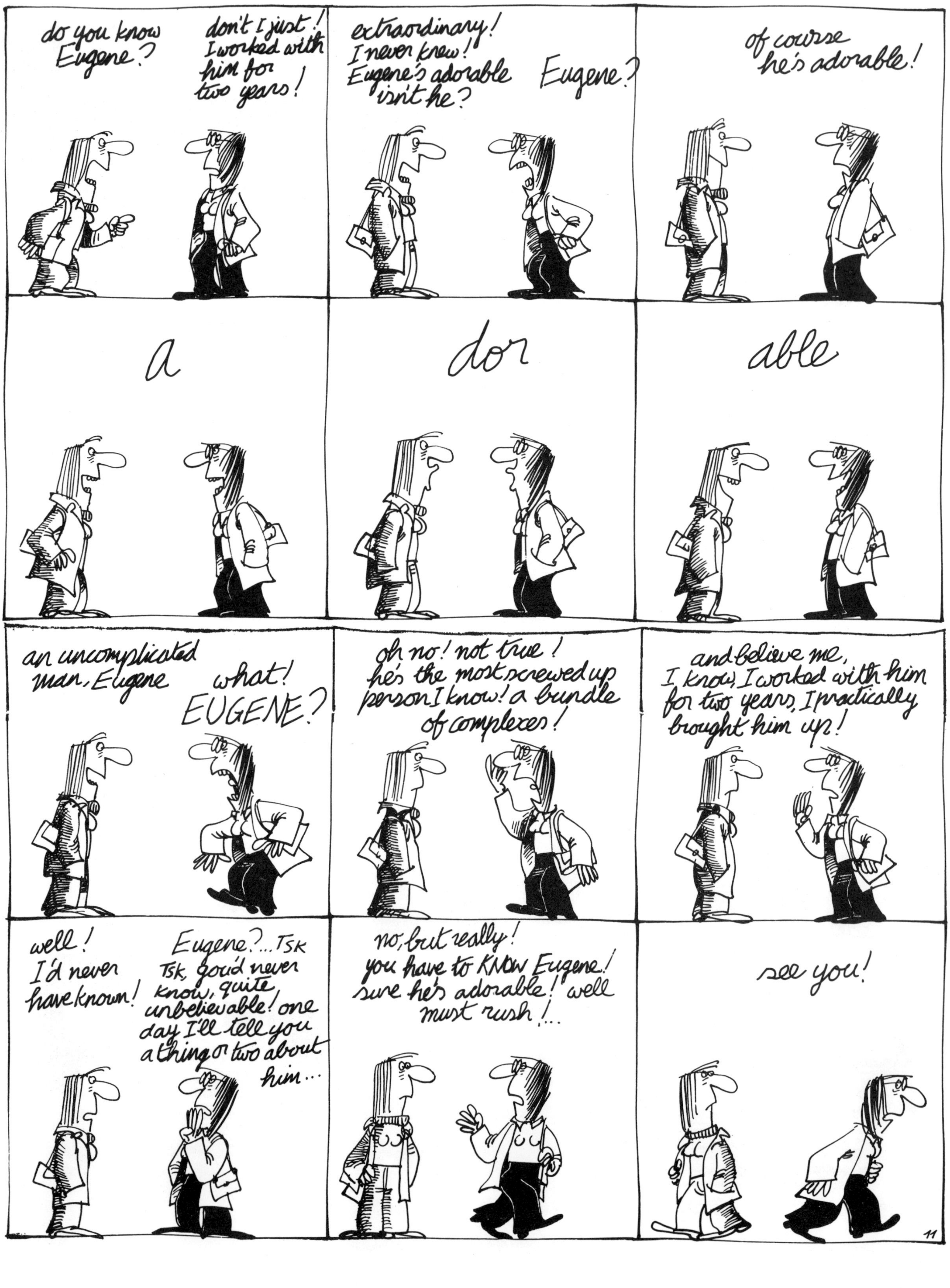

do you know Eugene?
don't I just! I worked with him for two years!
extraordinary! I never knew! Eugene's adorable isn't he?
Eugene?
of course he's adorable!
a
dor
able
an uncomplicated man, Eugene
what! EUGENE?
oh no! not true! he's the most screwed up person I know! a bundle of complexes!
and believe me, I know, I worked with him for two years, I practically brought him up!
well! I'd never have known!
Eugene?... Tsk Tsk, you'd never know, quite unbelievable! one day I'll tell you a thing or two about him...
no, but really! you have to KNOW Eugene! sure he's adorable! well must rush!...
see you!

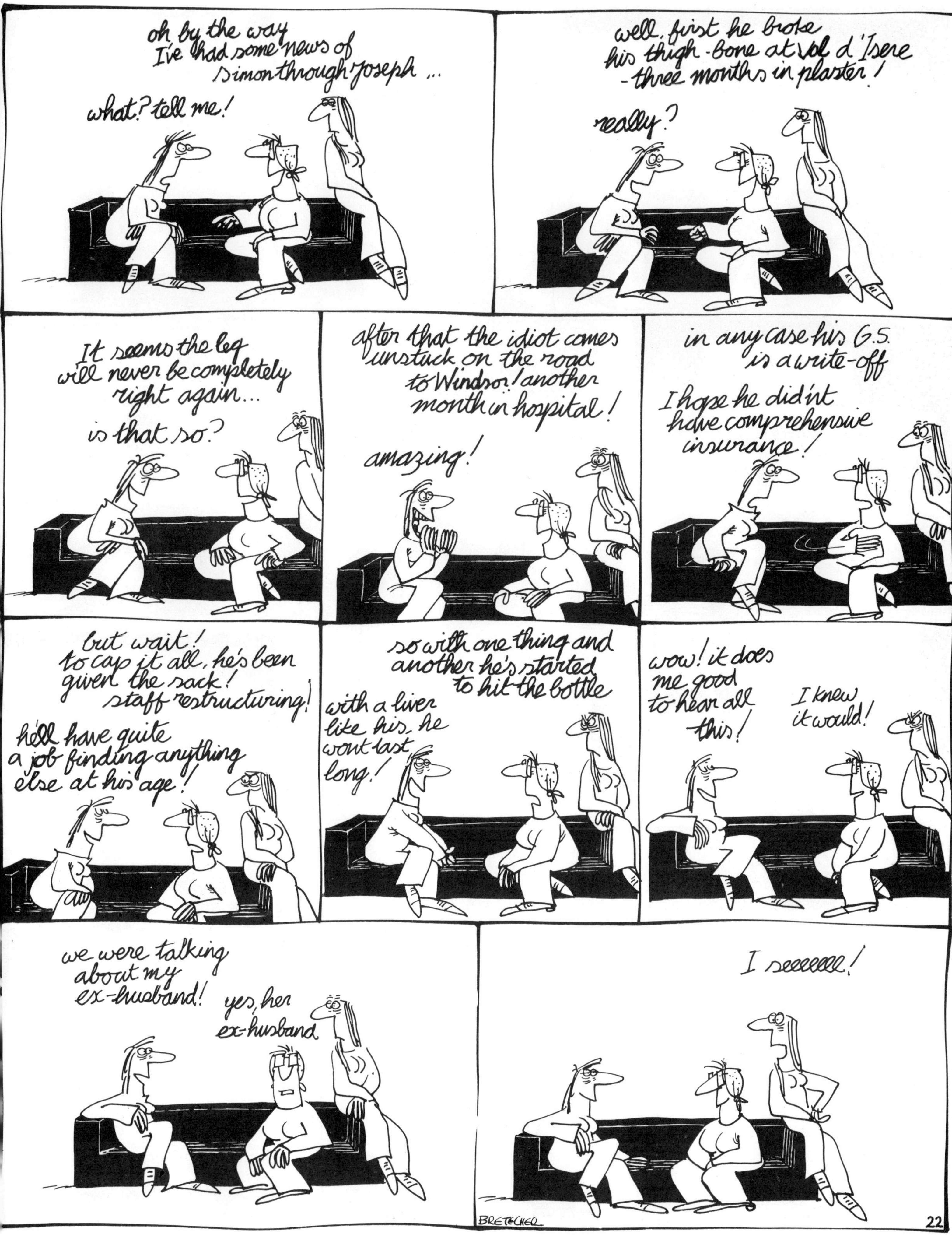
oh by the way I've had some news of simon through joseph ...
what? tell me!
well, first he broke his thigh-bone at Val d'Isere - three months in plaster!
really?
It seems the leg will never be completely right again...
is that so?
after that the idiot comes unstuck on the road to Windsor! another month in hospital!
amazing!
in any case his G.S. is a write-off
I hope he didn't have comprehensive insurance!
but wait! to cap it all, he's been given the sack! staff restructuring!
he'll have quite a job finding anything else at his age!
so with one thing and another he's started to hit the bottle
with a liver like his, he won't last long!
wow! it does me good to hear all this!
I knew it would!
we were talking about my ex-husband!
yes, her ex-husband
I seeeeee!
BRETECHER

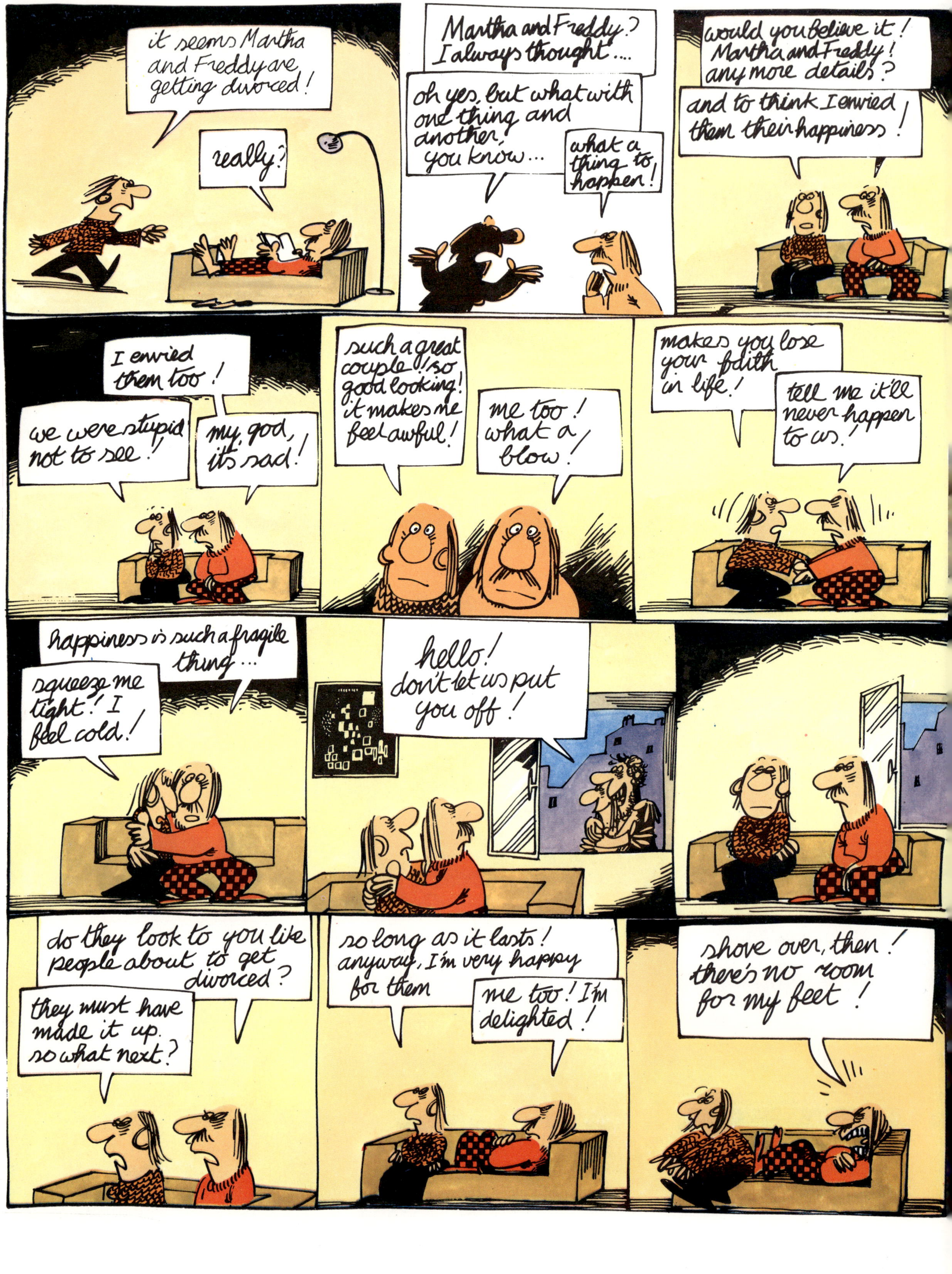
it seems Martha and Freddy are getting divorced!
really?
Martha and Freddy? I always thought....
oh yes, but what with one thing and another, you know...
what a thing to happen!
would you believe it! Martha and Freddy! any more details?
and to think I envied them their happiness!
I envied them too!
we were stupid not to see!
my god, it's sad!
such a great couple! so good looking! it makes me feel awful!
me too! what a blow!
makes you lose your faith in life!
tell me it'll never happen to us!
happiness is such a fragile thing...
squeeze me tight! I feel cold!
hello! don't let us put you off!
do they look to you like people about to get divorced?
they must have made it up. so what next?
so long as it lasts! anyway, I'm very happy for them
me too! I'm delighted!
shove over, then! there's no room for my feet!

my man

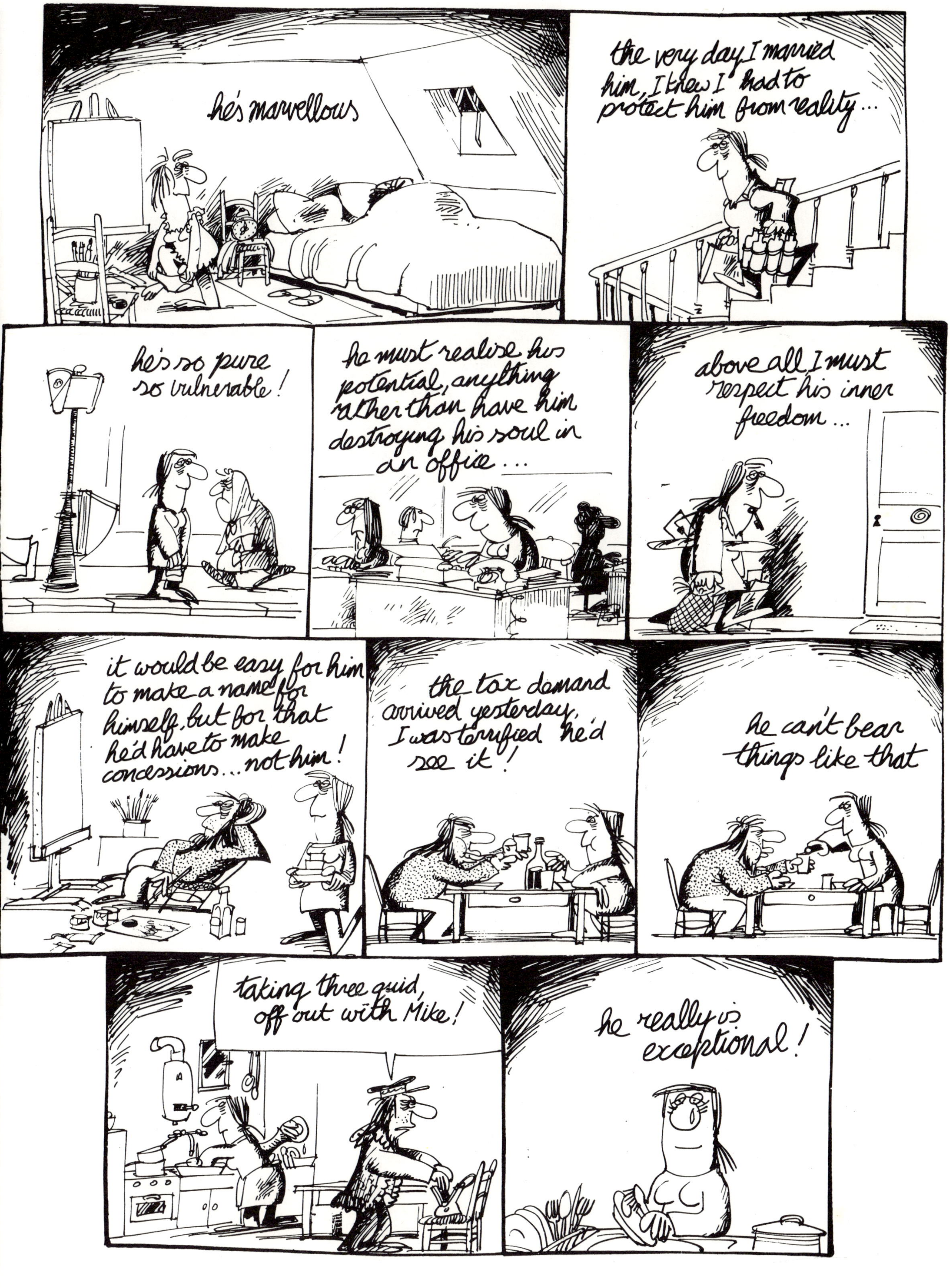

he's marvellous
the very day I married him, I knew I had to protect him from reality...
he's so pure so vulnerable!
he must realise his potential, anything rather than have him destroying his soul in an office...
above all I must respect his inner freedom...
it would be easy for him to make a name for himself, but for that he'd have to make concessions... not him!
the tax demand arrived yesterday, I was terrified he'd see it!
he can't bear things like that
taking three quid, off out with Mike!
he really is exceptional!

heart to heart

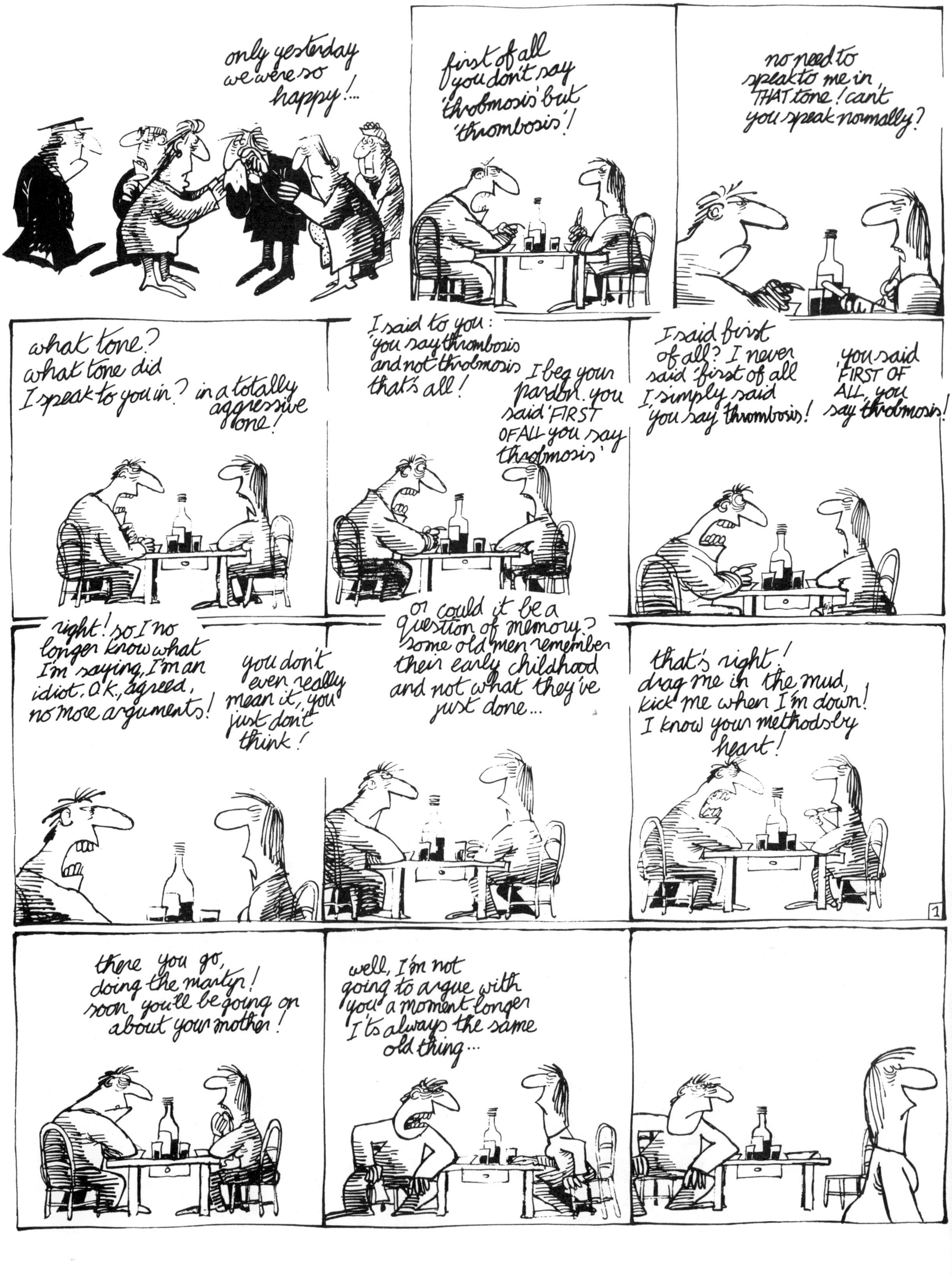
only yesterday we were so happy!...
first of all you don't say 'throbmosis' but 'thrombosis'!
no need to speak to me in THAT tone! can't you speak normally?
what tone? what tone did I speak to you in?
in a totally aggressive one!
I said to you: 'you say thrombosis and not throbmosis' that's all!
I beg your pardon. you said 'FIRST OF ALL you say throbmosis'
I said first of all? I never said 'first of all' I simply said 'you say thrombosis'!
you said 'FIRST OF ALL, you say throbmosis'!
right! so I no longer know what I'm saying, I'm an idiot, O.K., agreed, no more arguments!
you don't even really mean it, you just don't think!
or could it be a question of memory? some old men remember their early childhood and not what they've just done...
that's right! drag me in the mud, kick me when I'm down! I know your methods by heart!
1
there you go, doing the martyr! soon you'll be going on about your mother!
well, I'm not going to argue with you a moment longer. It's always the same old thing...

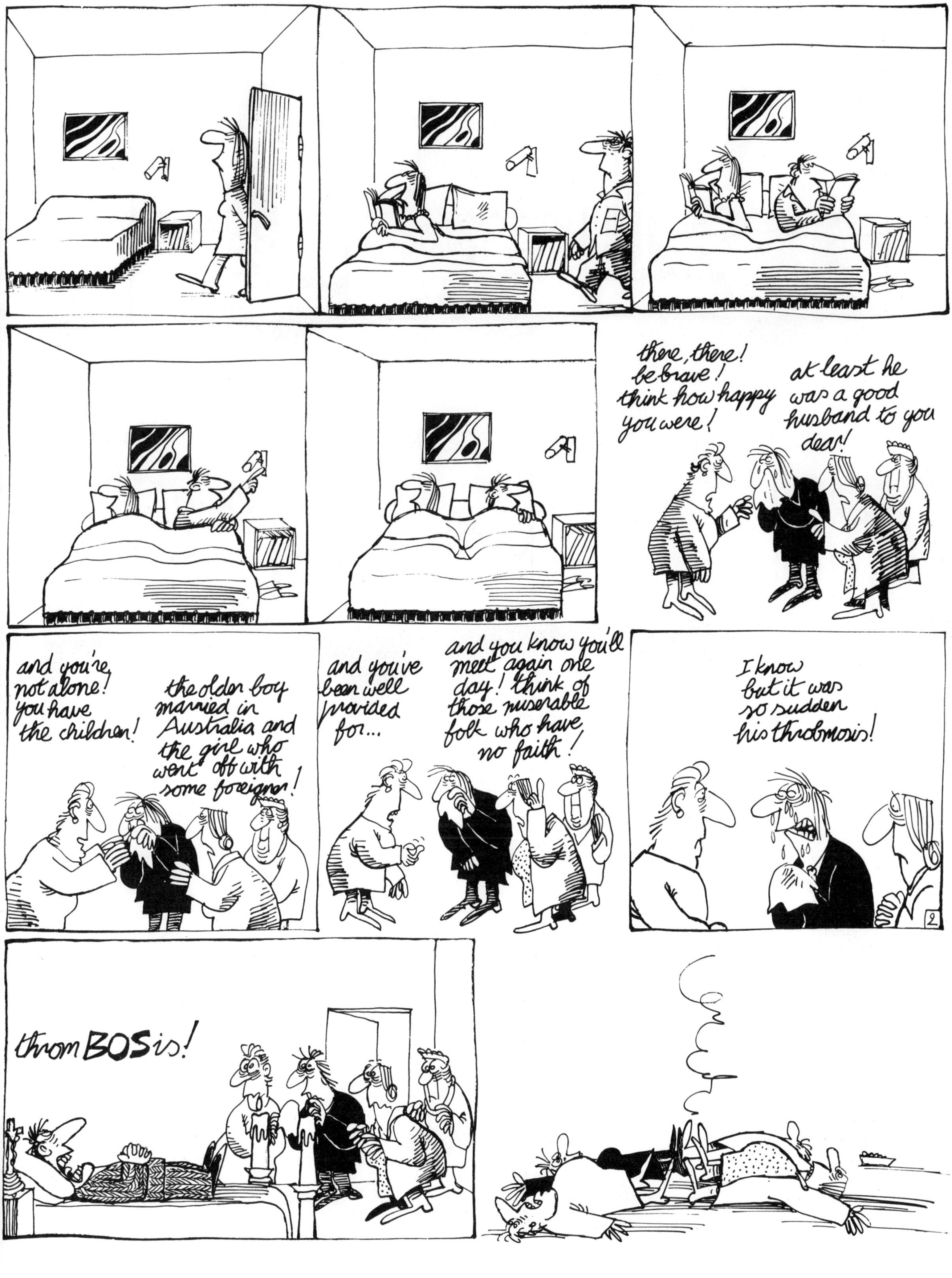
there, there! be brave! think how happy you were!
at least he was a good husband to you dear!
and you're not alone! you have the children!
the older boy married in Australia and the girl who went off with some foreigner!
and you've been well provided for...
and you know you'll meet again one day! think of those miserable folk who have no faith!
I know but it was so sudden his throbmosis!
2
thromBOSis!

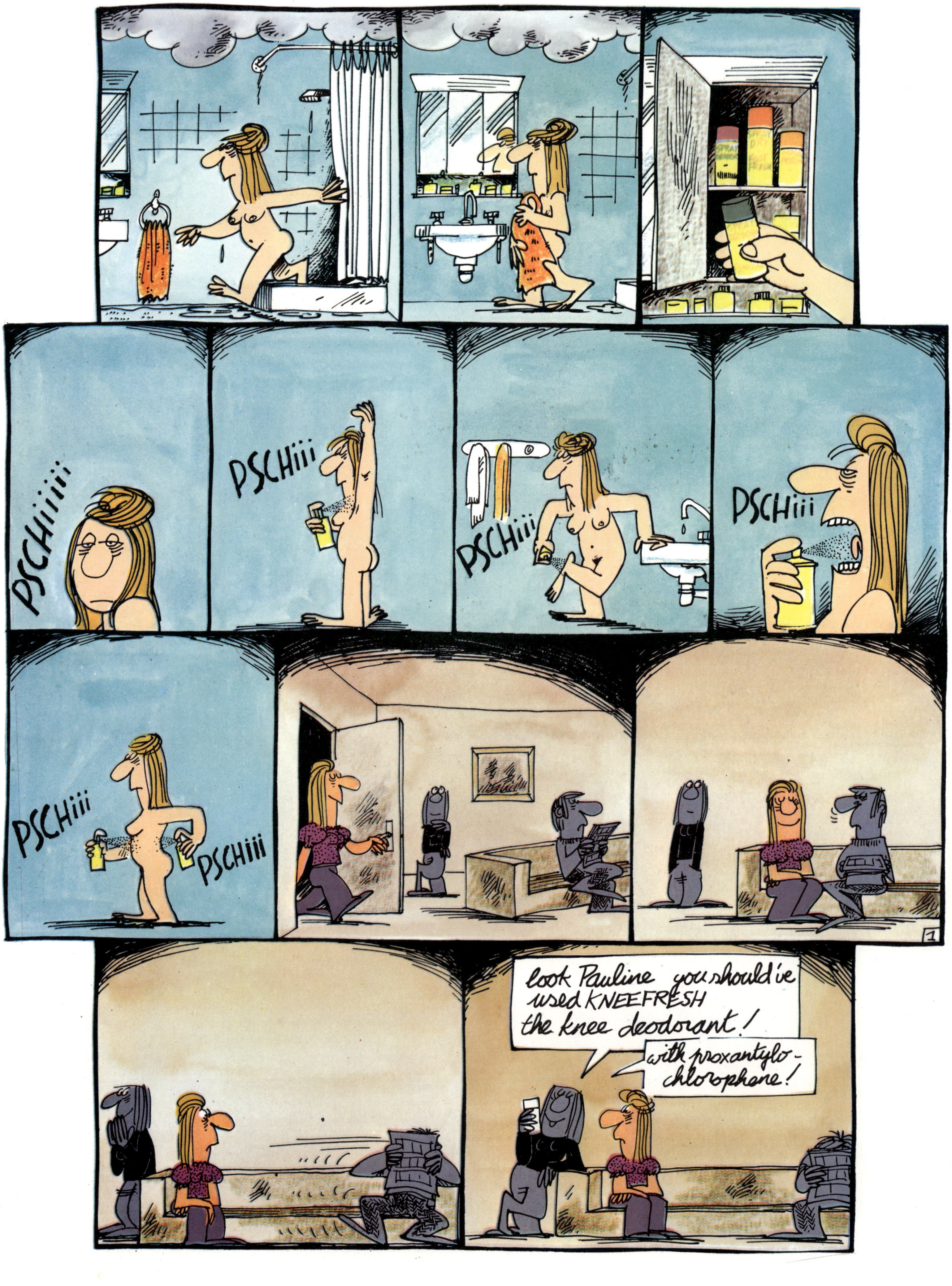
PSCHiiiiii
PSCHiii
PSCHiii
PSCHiii
PSCHiii
PSCHiii
1
look Pauline you should've used KNEEFRESH the knee deodorant!
with proxantylo-chlorophane!

CEMENT

The word 'cement' comes from the Latin COEMENTUM, the name give to the mixture of stone and lime mortar the Romans used for their buildings. If the Romans had used the word 'vinum' for this mixture, cement would not be called 'wine'; on the same principle, if the mixture had been christened 'tablinium', cement woud today be called 'table'. This kind of extrapolation can lead to a state of unease called vertigo, from the Latin 'Vertigo', which means cement.

Below: an example of vertigo produced by cement:

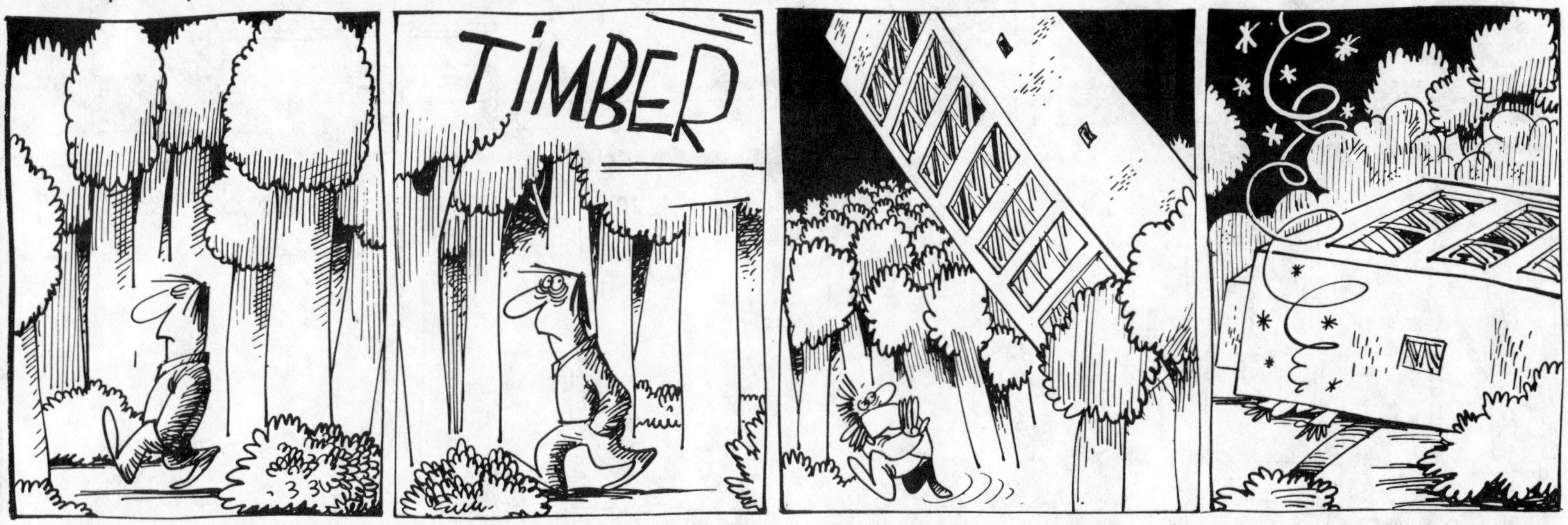
TIMBER

Cement was discovered in 1912 by the Frenchman Loulou-les-hernies, who used impure limestone.

Immediately a financier became interested in them and exploited them both (Loulou and the cement).

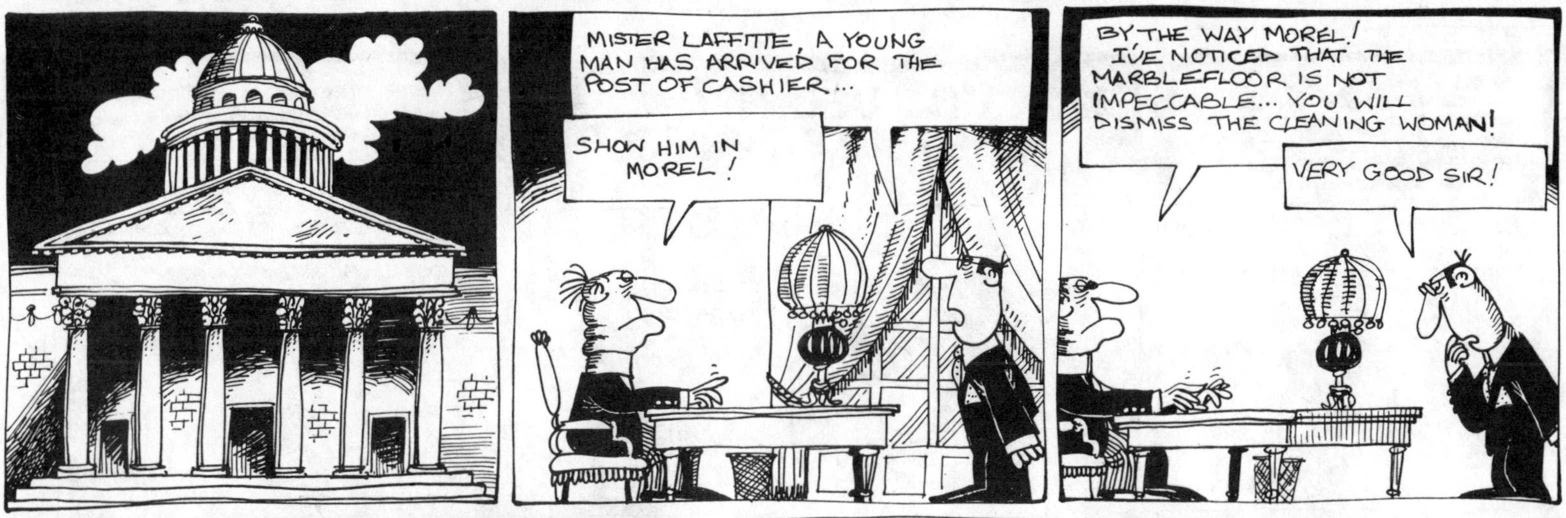
MISTER LAFFITTE, A YOUNG MAN HAS ARRIVED FOR THE POST OF CASHIER...
SHOW HIM IN MOREL!
BY THE WAY MOREL! I'VE NOTICED THAT THE MARBLEFLOOR IS NOT IMPECCABLE... YOU WILL DISMISS THE CLEANING WOMAN!
VERY GOOD SIR!

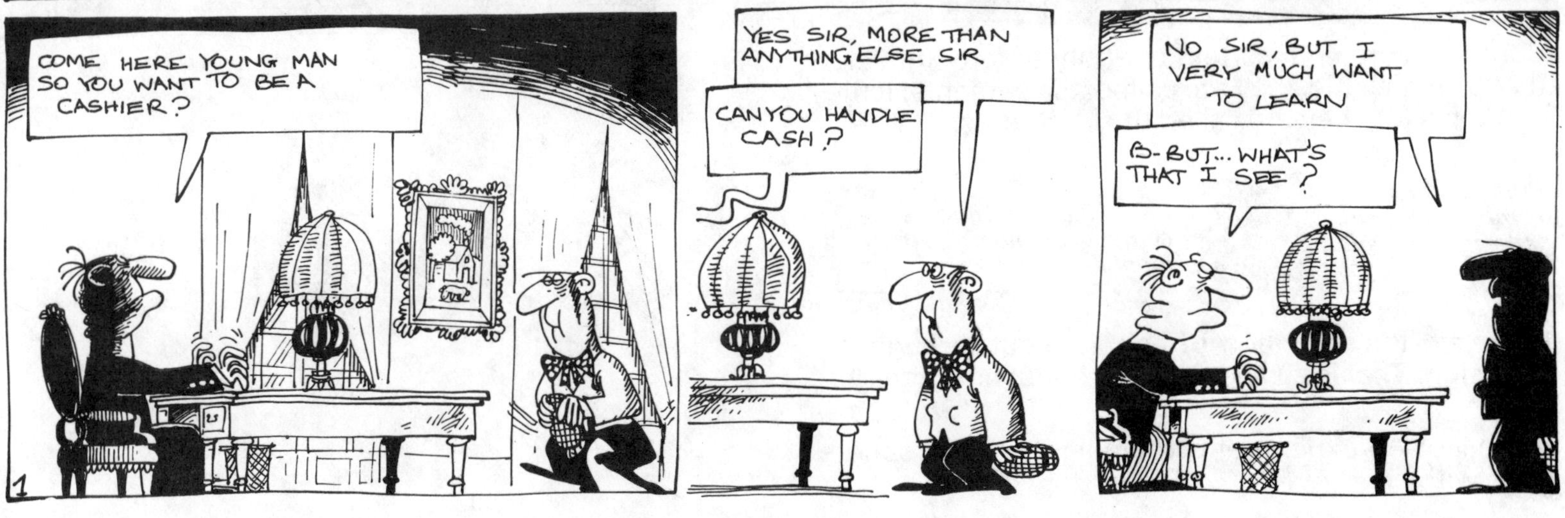
COME HERE YOUNG MAN SO YOU WANT TO BE A CASHIER?
YES SIR, MORE THAN ANYTHING ELSE SIR
CAN YOU HANDLE CASH?
NO SIR, BUT I VERY MUCH WANT TO LEARN
B-BUT... WHAT'S THAT I SEE?

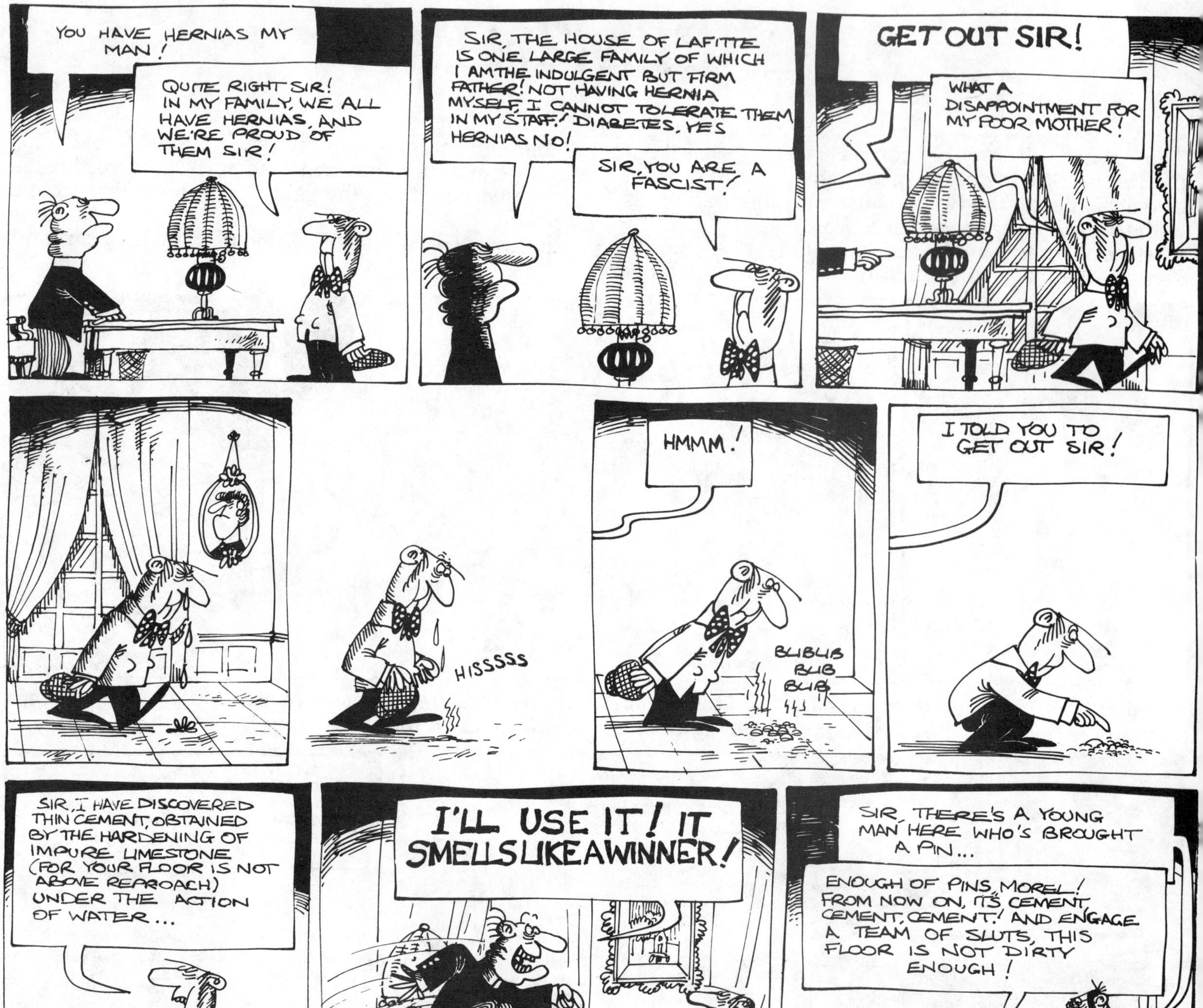
YOU HAVE HERNIAS MY MAN!
QUITE RIGHT SIR! IN MY FAMILY, WE ALL HAVE HERNIAS, AND WE'RE PROUD OF THEM SIR!
SIR, THE HOUSE OF LAFITTE IS ONE LARGE FAMILY OF WHICH I AM THE INDULGENT BUT FIRM FATHER! NOT HAVING HERNIA MYSELF, I CANNOT TOLERATE THEM IN MY STAFF! DIABETES, YES HERNIAS NO!
SIR, YOU ARE A FASCIST!
GET OUT SIR!
WHAT A DISAPPOINTMENT FOR MY POOR MOTHER!
HISSSSS
HMMM!
BLUBLUB BLUB BLUB
I TOLD YOU TO GET OUT SIR!
SIR, I HAVE DISCOVERED THIN CEMENT, OBTAINED BY THE HARDENING OF IMPURE LIMESTONE (FOR YOUR FLOOR IS NOT ABOVE REPROACH) UNDER THE ACTION OF WATER...
I'LL USE IT! IT SMELLS LIKE A WINNER!
SIR, THERE'S A YOUNG MAN HERE WHO'S BROUGHT A PIN...
ENOUGH OF PINS, MOREL! FROM NOW ON, IT'S CEMENT, CEMENT, CEMENT! AND ENGAGE A TEAM OF SLUTS, THIS FLOOR IS NOT DIRTY ENOUGH!

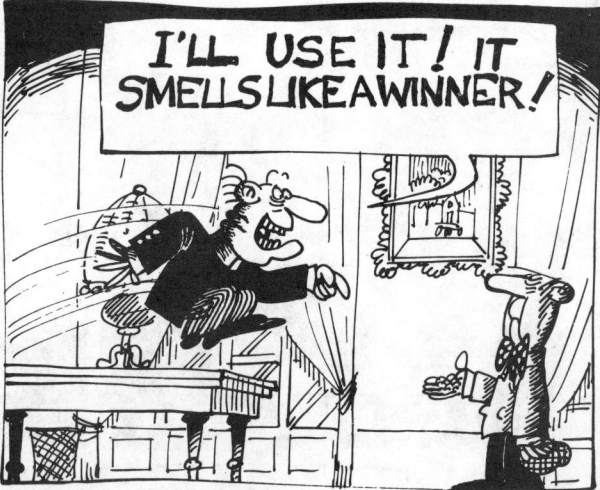

Cements contain a certain quantity of fatty matter. If they contain little, they are called thin cements; if they contain a lot, they are called thick cements.

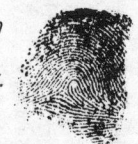

Print obtained with cement containing little greasy matter.

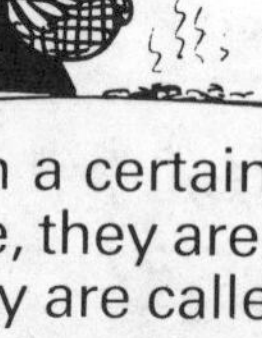

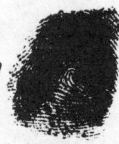

Print obtained with cement containing a lot of it.

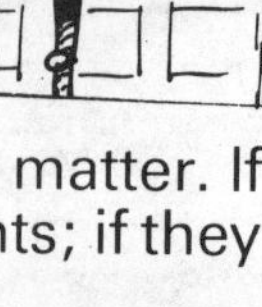

1910 saw the invention of light cement through air occlusion. That is all I have to say about light cement.

Opposite: An experiment with a light cement sphere filled with air.

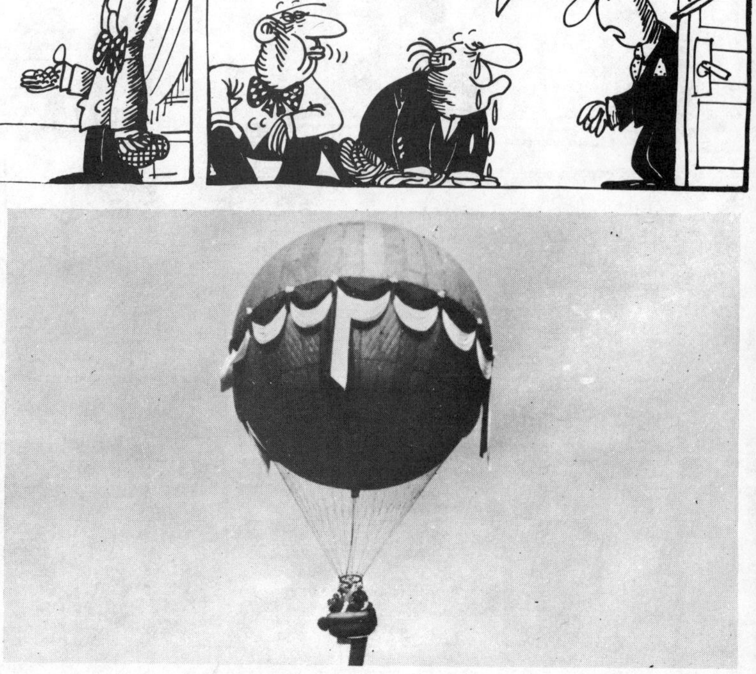

The foremost quality of cement is its solidity. Some builders prefer bricks. My, my! What a mistake!

Look at the two photographs below; wouldn't a good cement car have been better?

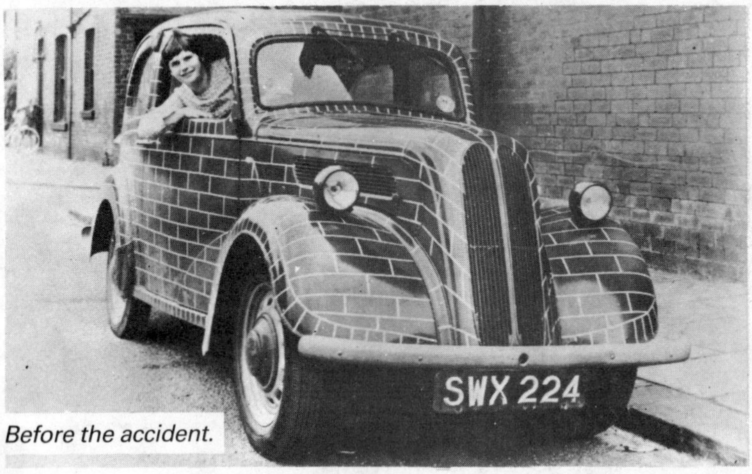
SWX 224
Before the accident.

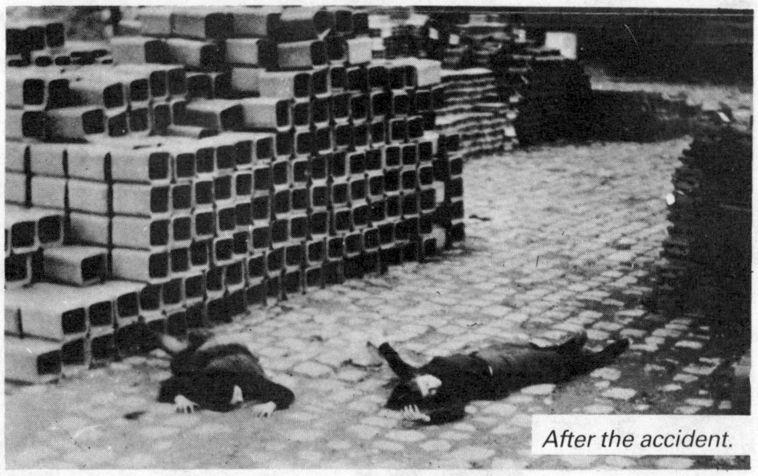
After the accident.

In 1920 appeared the first paper sacks for the packaging of cement (or vertigo). A modern packaging machine can fill 1200 sacks an hour.
1925 saw the first automated strike in the history of labour: a foreman in charge of sacking was distracted, and someone sacked the sackers instead of sacking the cement. Hence the strike. Since there were no sackers around to sack, all sacking stopped. The guilty foreman was condemned to death and to copy out two thousand times: 'She stacks cement sacks in the sacking store'

The pictures below show the sacked sackers shaking off their sacks.

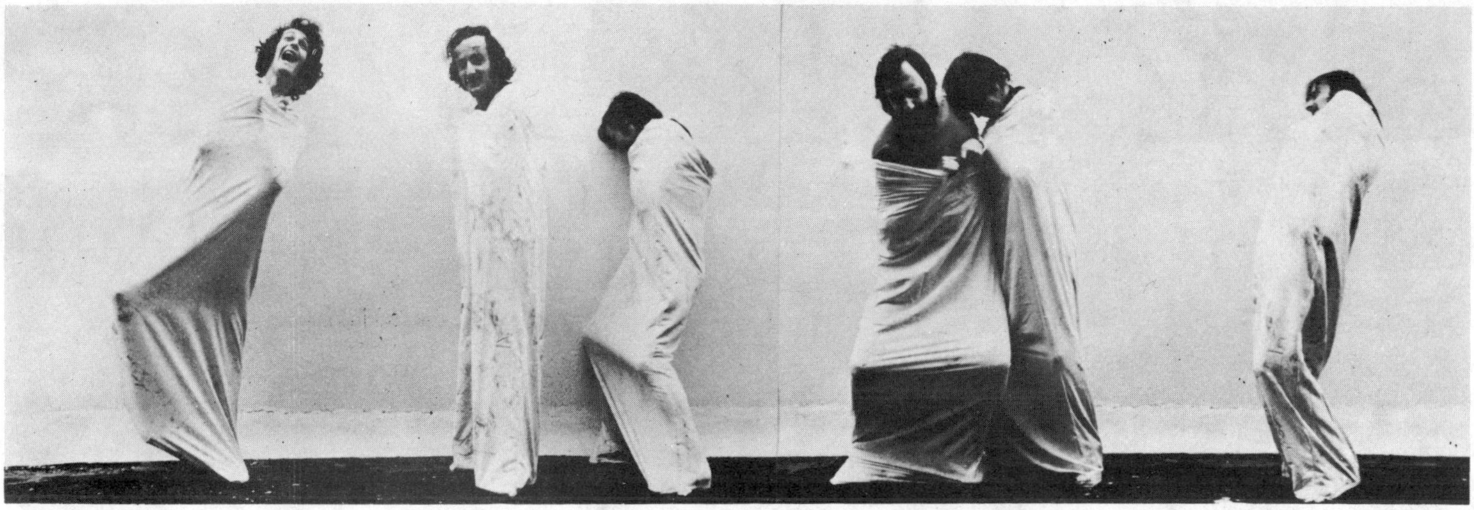

In 1970 the average annual consumption of cement per inhabitant in U.K. was in the region of 1,000 lbs.

People questioned in the Gallup poll revealed that they injected cement. Let us look the example of Mrs. P.

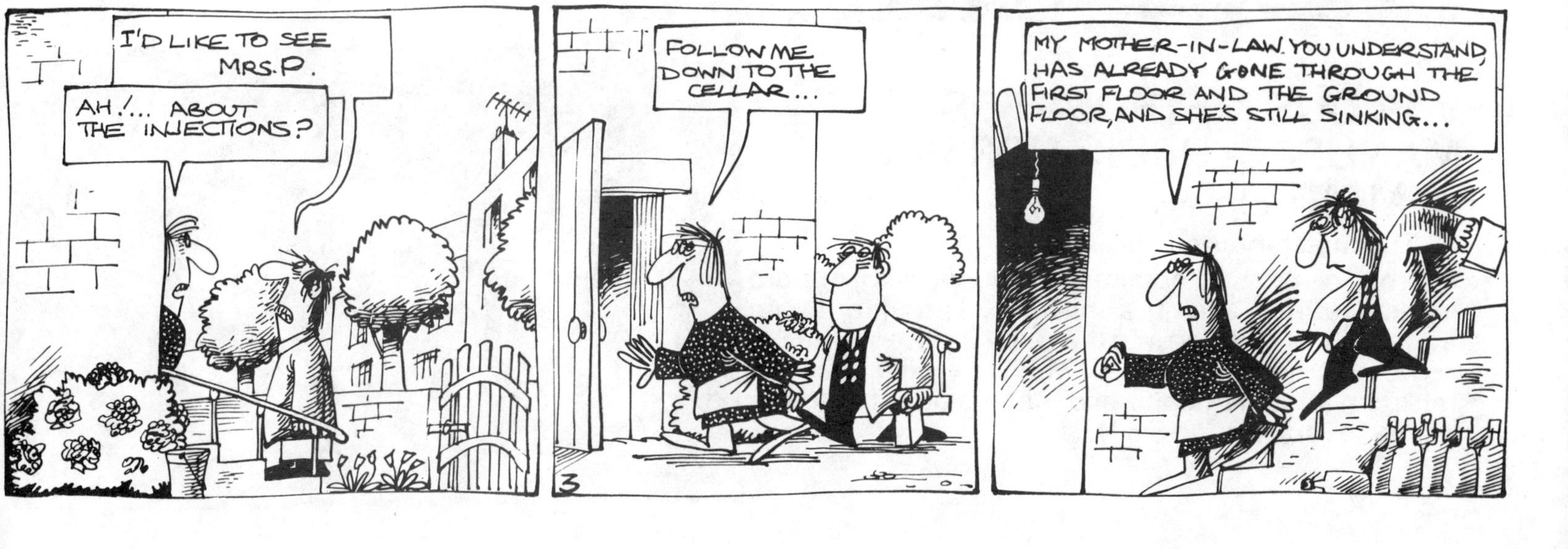
I'D LIKE TO SEE MRS. P.
AH!... ABOUT THE INJECTIONS?
FOLLOW ME DOWN TO THE CELLAR...
MY MOTHER-IN-LAW, YOU UNDERSTAND, HAS ALREADY GONE THROUGH THE FIRST FLOOR AND THE GROUND FLOOR, AND SHE'S STILL SINKING...

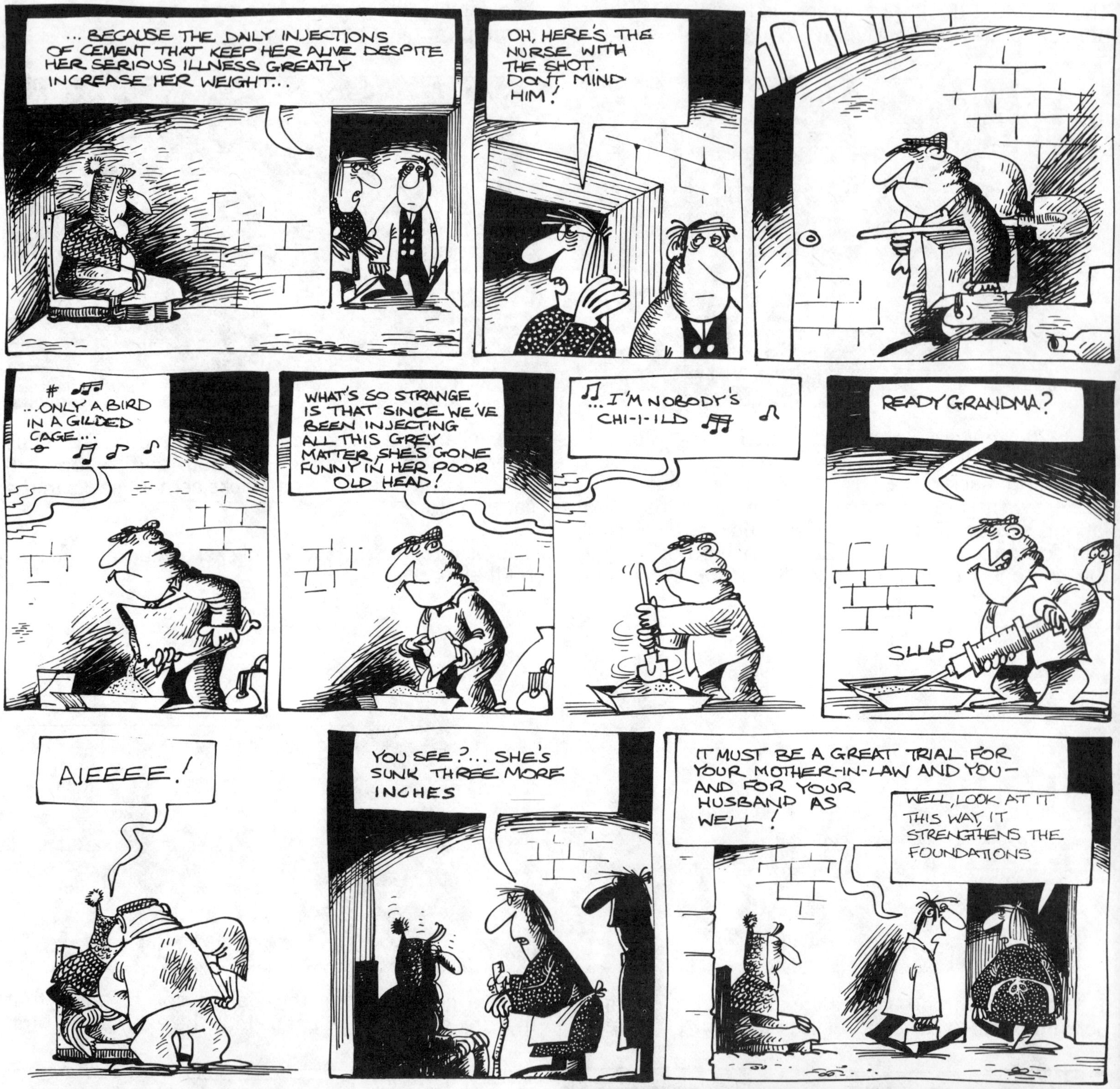
... BECAUSE THE DAILY INJECTIONS OF CEMENT THAT KEEP HER ALIVE DESPITE HER SERIOUS ILLNESS GREATLY INCREASE HER WEIGHT...
OH, HERE'S THE NURSE WITH THE SHOT. DON'T MIND HIM!
...ONLY A BIRD IN A GILDED CAGE...
WHAT'S SO STRANGE IS THAT SINCE WE'VE BEEN INJECTING ALL THIS GREY MATTER SHE'S GONE FUNNY IN HER POOR OLD HEAD!
...I'M NOBODY'S CHI-I-ILD
READY GRANDMA?
SLLLP
AIEEEE!
YOU SEE?... SHE'S SUNK THREE MORE INCHES
IT MUST BE A GREAT TRIAL FOR YOUR MOTHER-IN-LAW AND YOU— AND FOR YOUR HUSBAND AS WELL!
WELL, LOOK AT IT THIS WAY, IT STRENGTHENS THE FOUNDATIONS

VARIOUS METHODS FOR MANUFACTURING NORMAL CEMENT (Or vertigo)

a) **The moist method**:

Normal cement is obtained by pulverizing impure limestone, and adding a milkman. The unfortunate tradesman is plunged into the blast-furnace where the cement is heated. It goes without saying that the milkman's family is plunged into a state of extreme grief and moisture. Fig. 1.

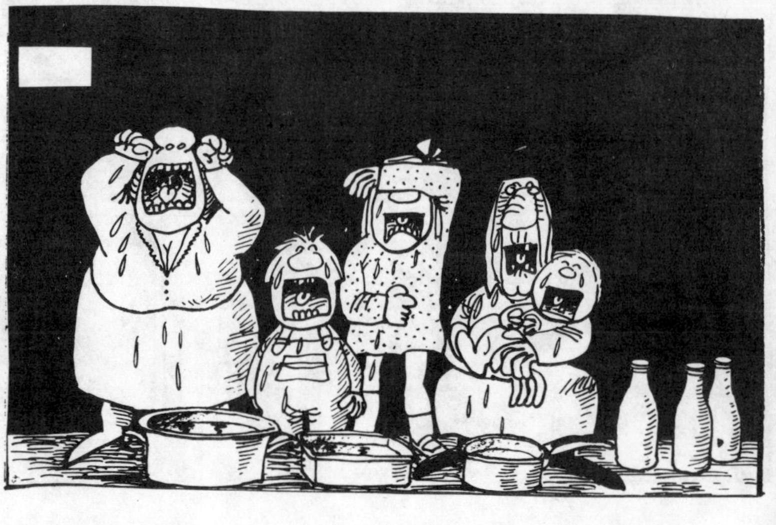

b) **The semi-moist method**:
The milkman's family has been generously compensated, thus lessening grief and moisture. Fig. 2.

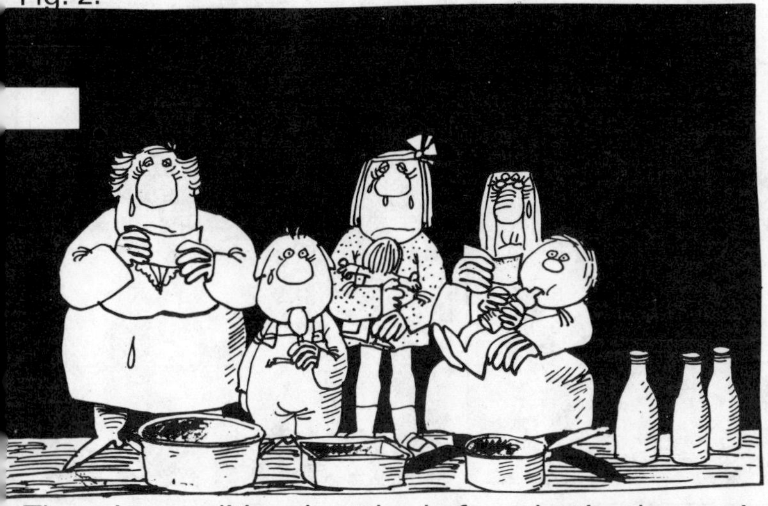

There is a traditional method of production known in the cement industry as 'spit-and-run'. Below we see a master spitter about to give a demonstration to his attentive apprentices.

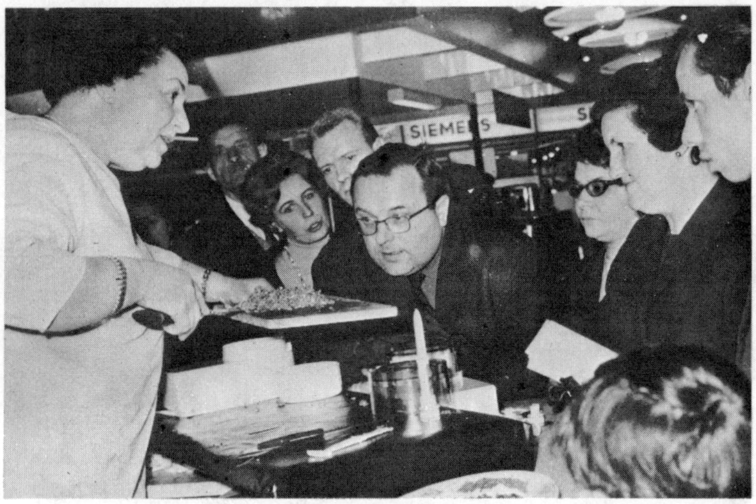

Cement may also be reinforced. Below, some concrete examples of this method.

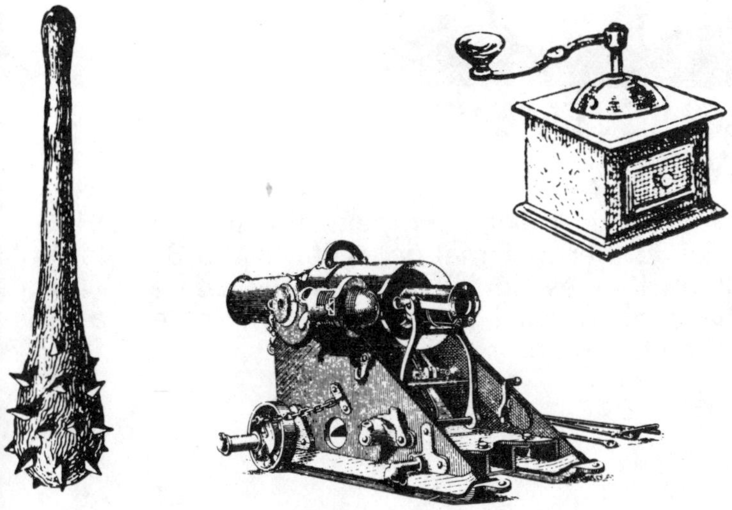

c) **The dry method**:
Use an orphan milkman. Fig. 3.

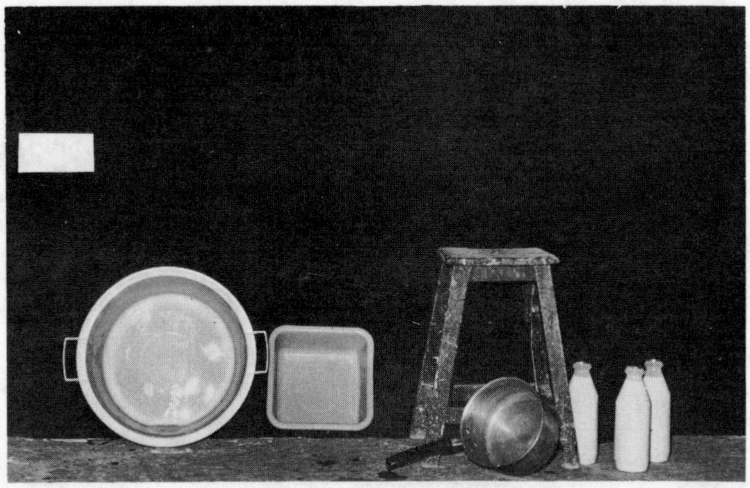

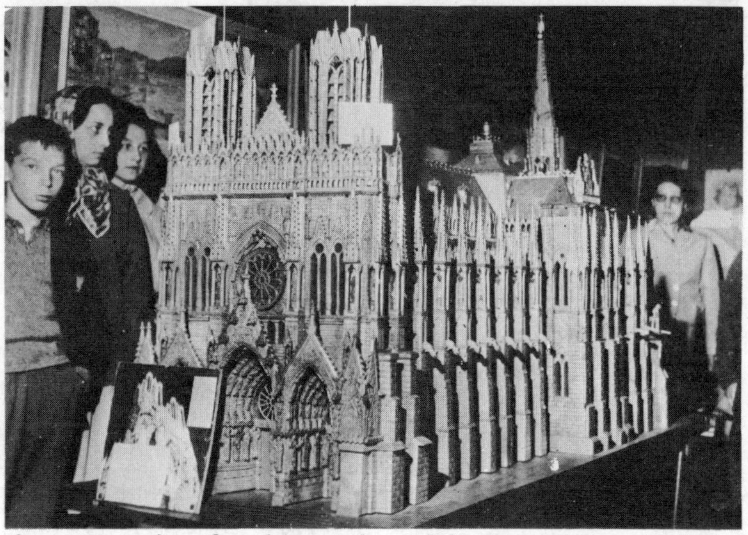

An example of a decorative object made entirely by the 'spit-and-run' method. It needed two thousand man-hours and 17 hogsheads of sterile saliva.

Heatproof cement air-conditioned shoes for American astronauts are also made by the 'spit-and-run' method. Opposite, a batch being dried prior to running.

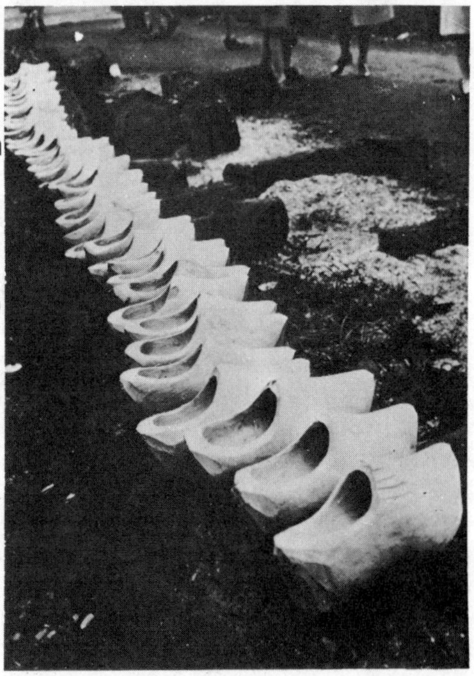

An extract from 'Cement was waiting' by Arnold Pinter, with Arnold playing the milkman's son.

It was over this film that Arnold had a quarrel with his father Albert in the course of which Albert uttered the famous phrase: 'Tu quoque, mi fili', which could be translated as: 'Cement to you!'

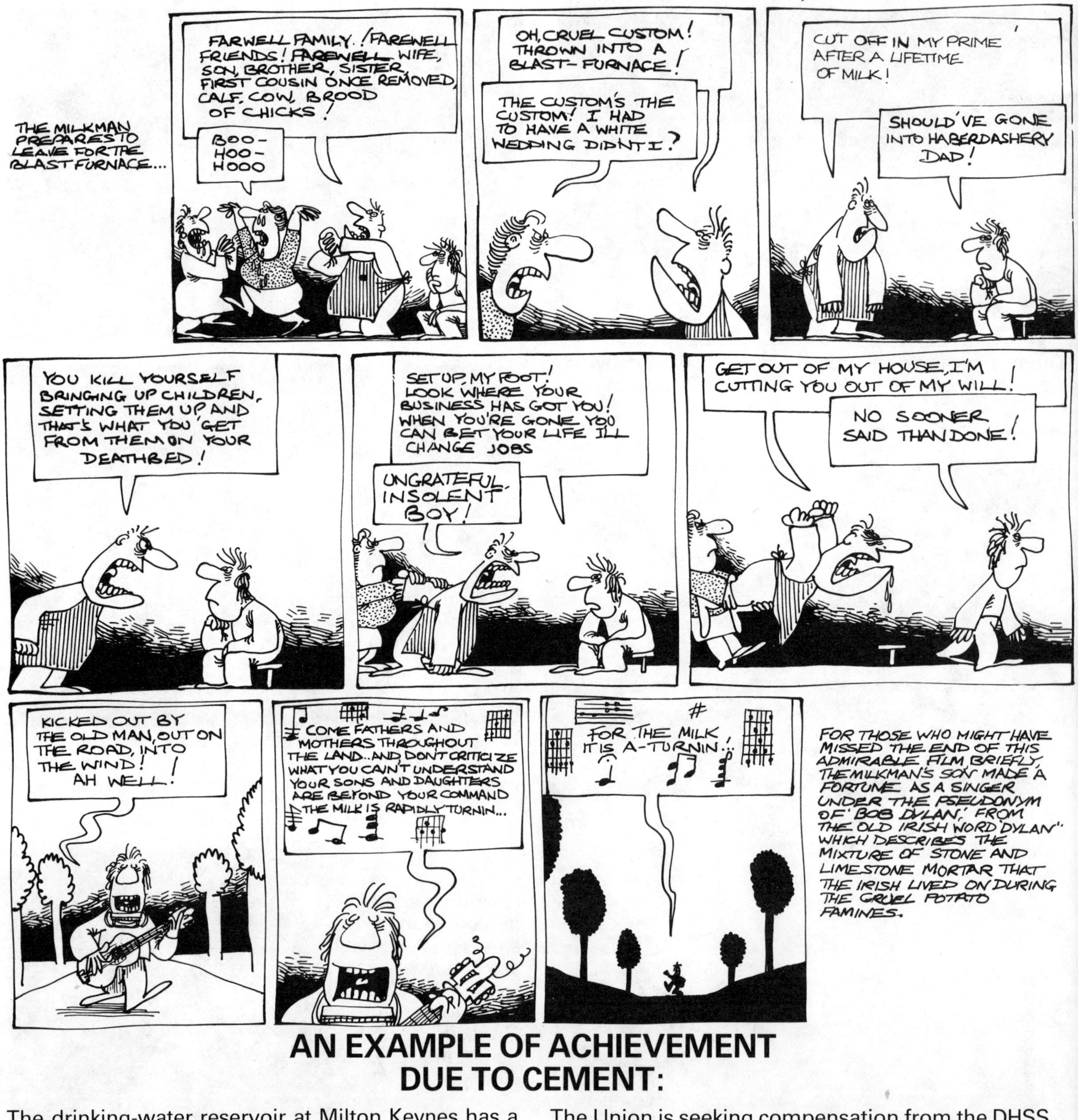

THE MILKMAN PREPARES TO LEAVE FOR THE BLAST FURNACE...
FARWELL FAMILY! FAREWELL FRIENDS! FAREWELL WIFE, SON, BROTHER, SISTER, FIRST COUSIN ONCE REMOVED, CALF, COW, BROOD OF CHICKS!
BOO-HOO-HOOO
OH, CRUEL CUSTOM! THROWN INTO A BLAST-FURNACE!
THE CUSTOM'S THE CUSTOM! I HAD TO HAVE A WHITE WEDDING DIDN'T I?
CUT OFF IN MY PRIME AFTER A LIFETIME OF MILK!
SHOULD'VE GONE INTO HABERDASHERY DAD!
YOU KILL YOURSELF BRINGING UP CHILDREN, SETTING THEM UP AND THAT'S WHAT YOU GET FROM THEM ON YOUR DEATHBED!
SET UP, MY FOOT! LOOK WHERE YOUR BUSINESS HAS GOT YOU! WHEN YOU'RE GONE YOU CAN BET YOUR LIFE I'LL CHANGE JOBS
UNGRATEFUL, INSOLENT BOY!
GET OUT OF MY HOUSE, I'M CUTTING YOU OUT OF MY WILL!
NO SOONER SAID THAN DONE!
KICKED OUT BY THE OLD MAN, OUT ON THE ROAD, INTO THE WIND! AH WELL!
COME FATHERS AND MOTHERS THROUGHOUT THE LAND... AND DON'T CRITICIZE WHAT YOU CAN'T UNDERSTAND YOUR SONS AND DAUGHTERS ARE BEYOND YOUR COMMAND THE MILK IS RAPIDLY TURNIN...
FOR THE MILK IT IS A-TURNIN...
FOR THOSE WHO MIGHT HAVE MISSED THE END OF THIS ADMIRABLE FILM BRIEFLY, THE MILKMAN'S SON MADE A FORTUNE AS A SINGER UNDER THE PSEUDONYM OF 'BOB DYLAN,' FROM THE OLD IRISH WORD 'DYLAN' WHICH DESCRIBES THE MIXTURE OF STONE AND LIMESTONE MORTAR THAT THE IRISH LIVED ON DURING THE CRUEL POTATO FAMINES.

AN EXAMPLE OF ACHIEVEMENT DUE TO CEMENT:

The drinking-water reservoir at Milton Keynes has a capacity of 200,000 cubic feet. It consists of two watertight concrete tanks.

200 milkmen were required for each tank. Protesting against the demands made on its members, the Milkmens' Union has declared: 'We'll crack British Cement!'

The union leader was thrown into a blast furnace. The Union is seeking compensation from the DHSS.

For further information, write to the Secretary of Milton Keynes Social Services and Cement Works. That's about all I have to say on cement at this moment in time.

Kisses,
C.B.

happiness

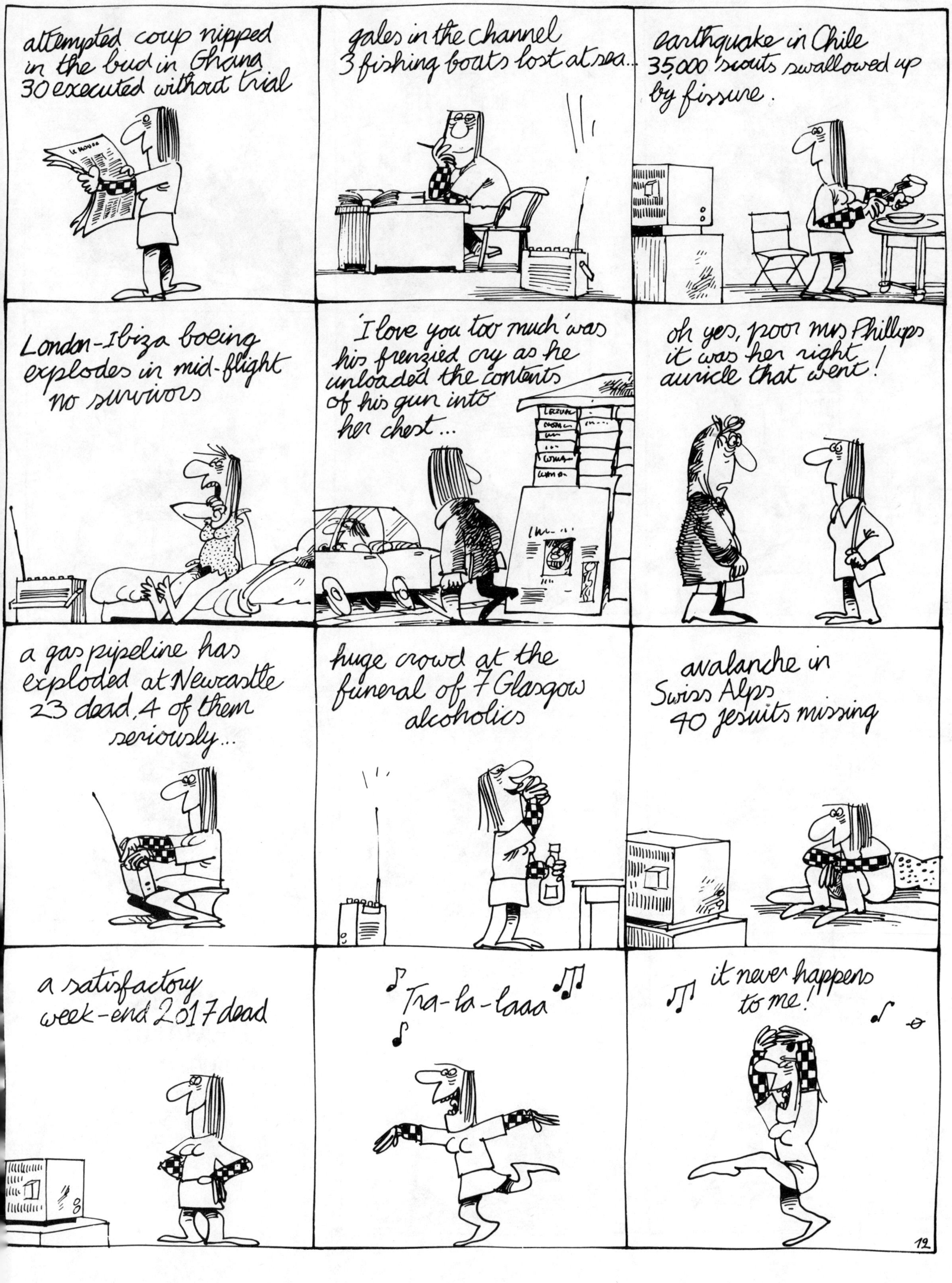
attempted coup nipped in the bud in Ghana 30 executed without trial
gales in the channel 3 fishing boats lost at sea...
earthquake in Chile 35,000 scouts swallowed up by fissure.
London-Ibiza boeing explodes in mid-flight no survivors
'I love you too much' was his frenzied cry as he unloaded the contents of his gun into her chest...
oh yes, poor mrs Phillips it was her right auricle that went!
a gas pipeline has exploded at Newcastle 23 dead, 4 of them seriously...
huge crowd at the funeral of 7 Glasgow alcoholics
avalanche in Swiss Alps 40 jesuits missing
a satisfactory week-end 2017 dead
Tra-la-laaa
it never happens to me!

the anxieties of Mrs Sugden

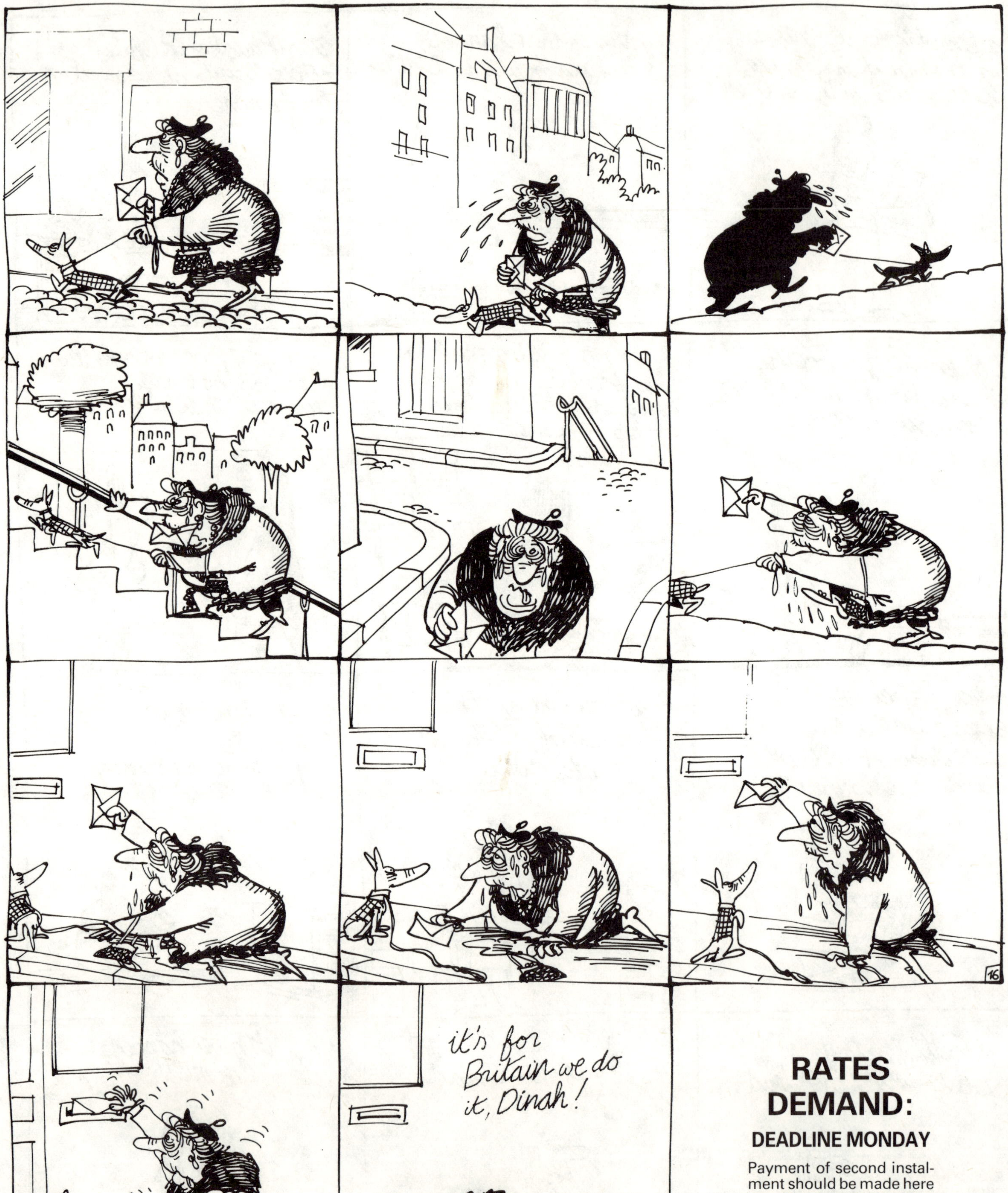

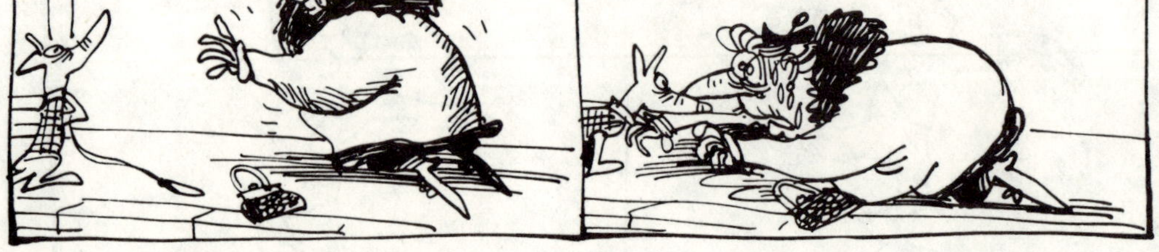
it's for Britain we do it, Dinah!

RATES DEMAND:

DEADLINE MONDAY

Payment of second instalment should be made here by Monday 15th May. From 16th May, a 10% increase will be chargeable on late payment.

the good wives of Paris

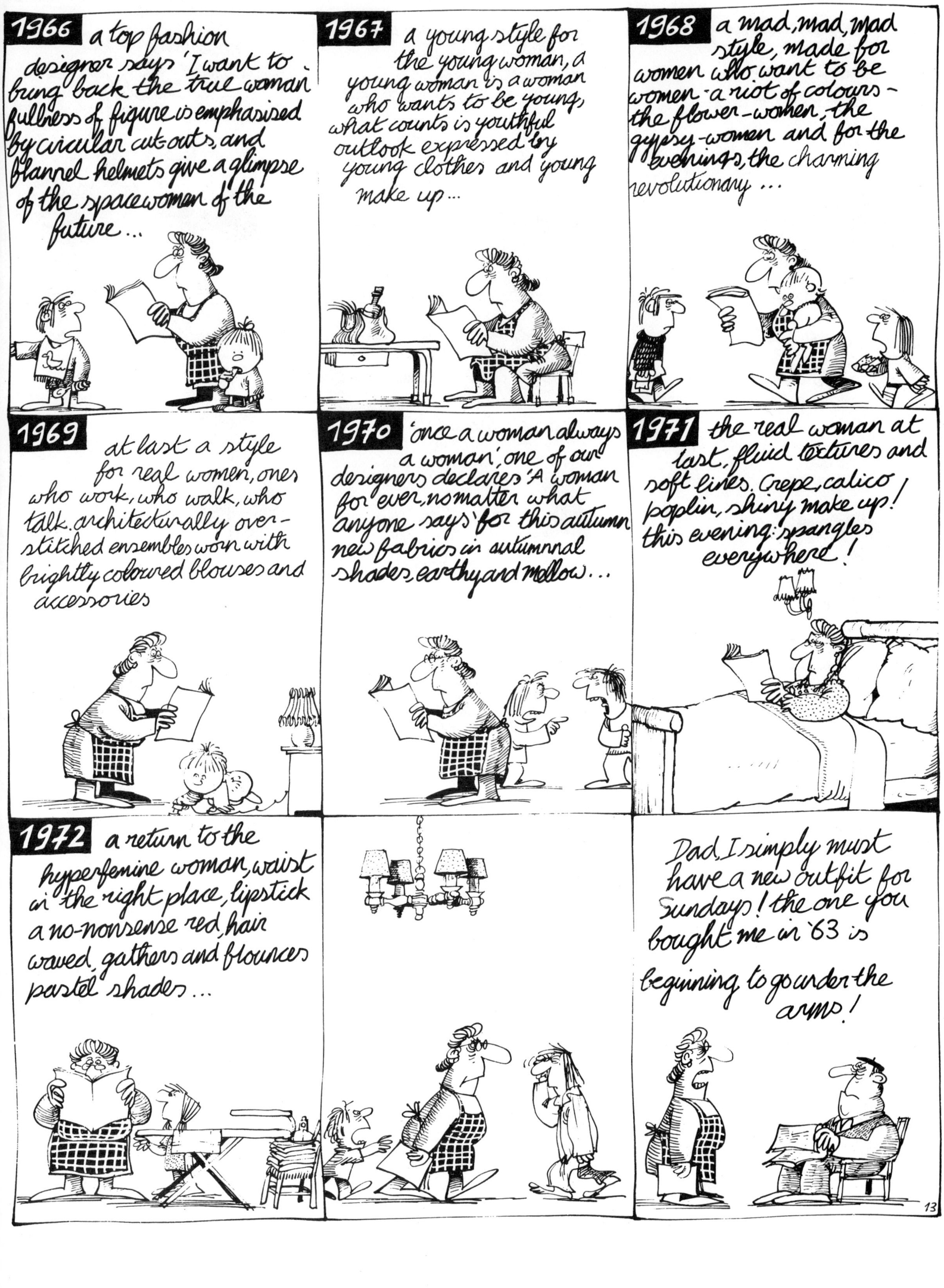

1966
a top fashion designer says 'I want to bring back the true woman' fullness of figure is emphasised by circular cut-outs, and flannel helmets give a glimpse of the spacewoman of the future...
1967
a young style for the young woman, a young woman is a woman who wants to be young, what counts is youthful outlook expressed by young clothes and young make up...
1968
a mad, mad, mad style, made for women who want to be women - a riot of colours - the flower-women, the gypsy-women and for the evenings, the charming revolutionary...
1969
at last a style for real women, ones who work, who walk, who talk. architecturally over-stitched ensembles worn with brightly coloured blouses and accessories
1970
'once a woman always a woman' one of our designers declares 'A woman for ever, no matter what anyone says' for this autumn new fabrics in autumnal shades, earthy and mellow...
1971
the real woman at last, fluid textures and soft lines. Crepe, calico poplin, shiny make up! this evening: spangles everywhere!
1972
a return to the hyperfemine woman, waist in the right place, lipstick a no-nonsense red, hair waved, gathers and flounces pastel shades...
Dad, I simply must have a new outfit for Sundays! the one you bought me in '63 is beginning to go under the arms!

to have and to have not

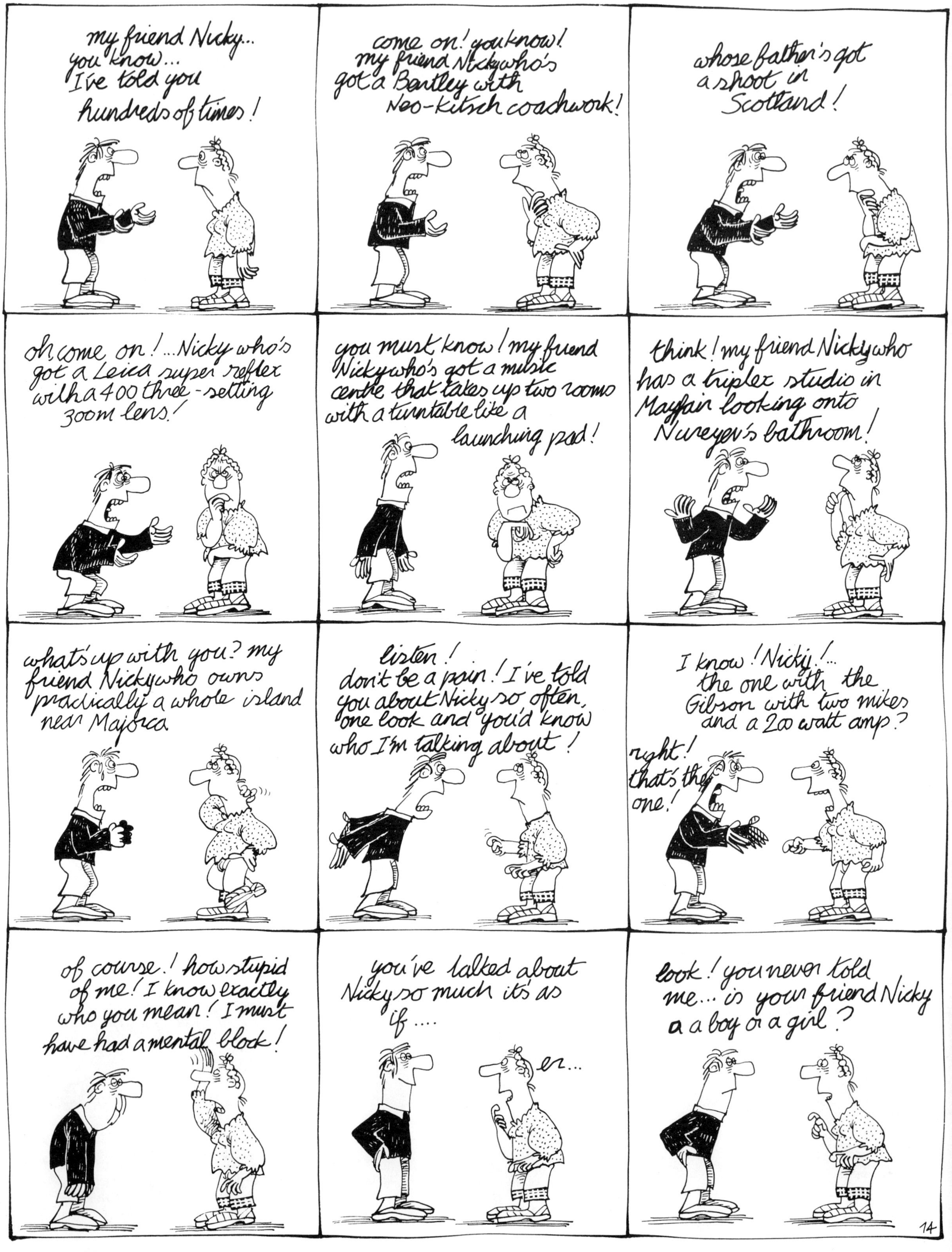

my friend Nicky... you know... I've told you hundreds of times!
come on! you know! my friend Nicky who's got a Bentley with Neo-Kitsch coachwork!
whose father's got a shoot in Scotland!
oh, come on! ...Nicky who's got a Leica super reflex with a 400 three-setting zoom lens!
you must know! my friend Nicky who's got a music centre that takes up two rooms with a turntable like a launching pad!
think! my friend Nicky who has a triplex studio in Mayfair looking onto Nureyev's bathroom!
what's up with you? my friend Nicky who owns practically a whole island near Majorca
listen! don't be a pain! I've told you about Nicky so often, one look and you'd know who I'm talking about!
I know! Nicky!... the one with the Gibson with two mikes and a 200 watt amp?
right! that's the one!
of course! how stupid of me! I know exactly who you mean! I must have had a mental block!
you've talked about Nicky so much it's as if ....
er...
look! you never told me... is your friend Nicky a a boy or a girl?

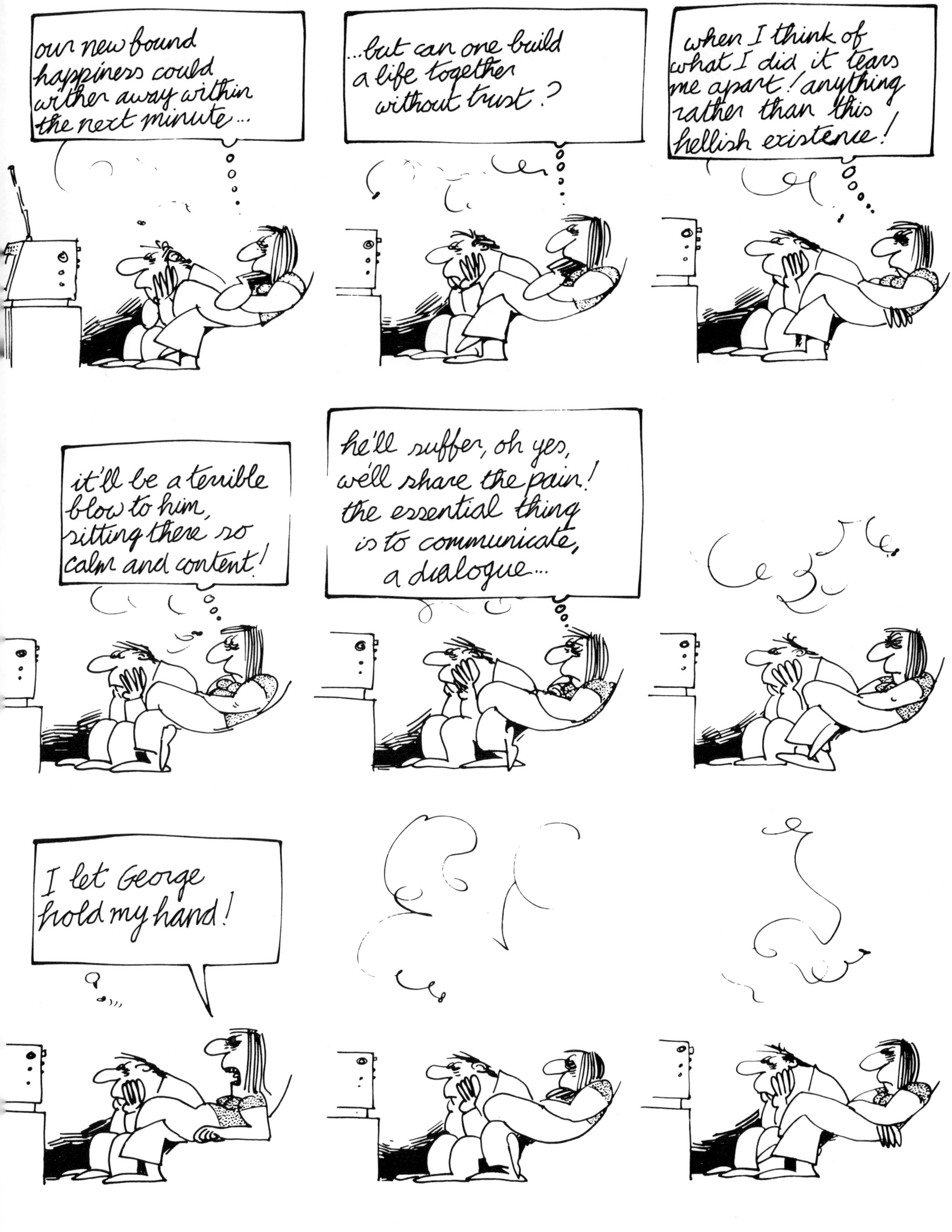
our new found happiness could wither away within the next minute...
...but can one build a life together without trust?
when I think of what I did it tears me apart! anything rather than this hellish existence!
it'll be a terrible blow to him, sitting there so calm and content!
he'll suffer, oh yes, we'll share the pain! the essential thing is to communicate, a dialogue...
I let George hold my hand!

theory and practice

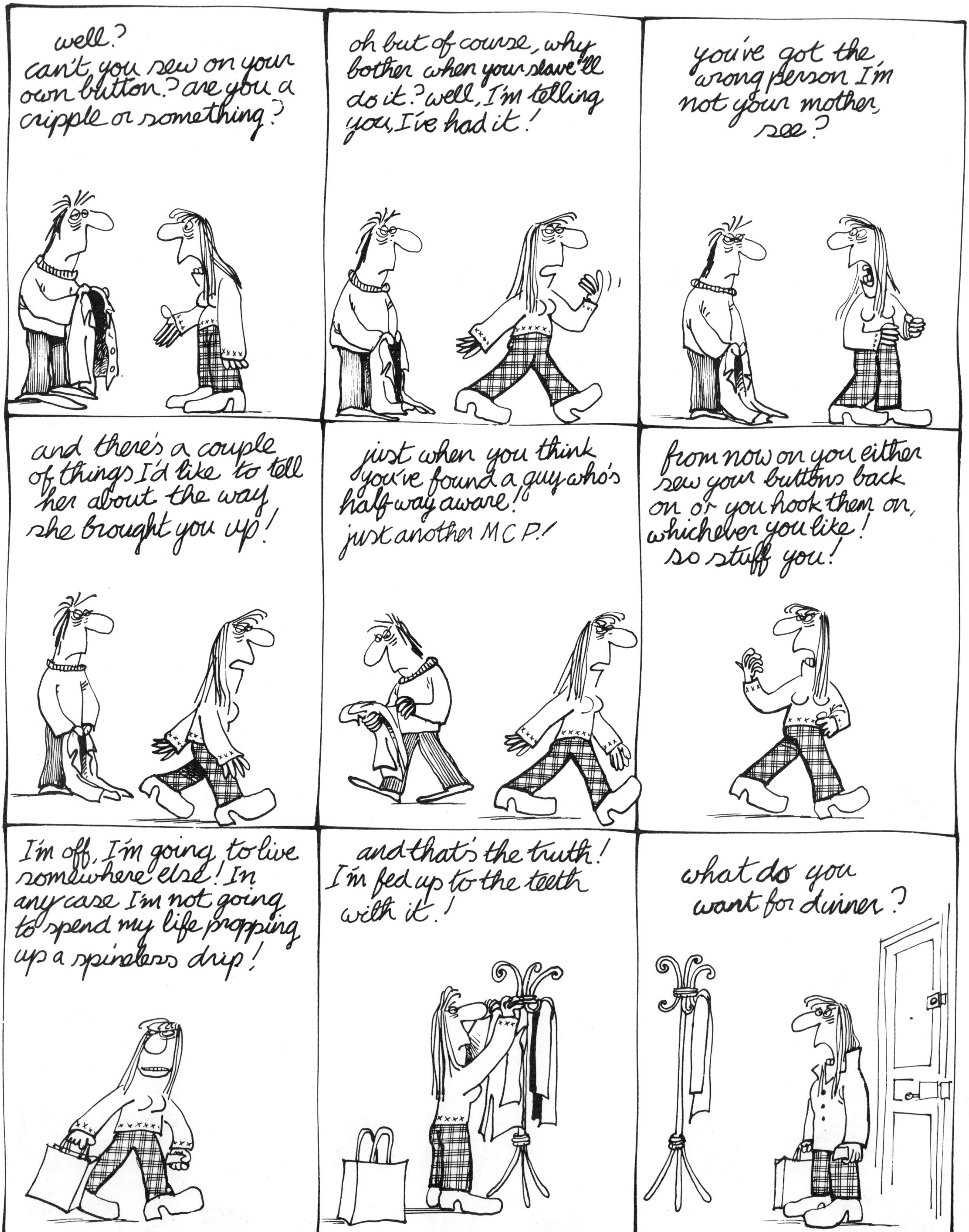
well? can't you sew on your own button? are you a cripple or something?
oh but of course, why bother when your slave'll do it? well, I'm telling you, I've had it!
you've got the wrong person I'm not your mother, see?
and there's a couple of things I'd like to tell her about the way she brought you up!
just when you think you've found a guy who's half-way aware! just another MCP!
from now on you either sew your buttons back on or you hook them on, whichever you like! so stuff you!
I'm off, I'm going to live somewhere else! In any case I'm not going to spend my life propping up a spineless drip!
and that's the truth! I'm fed up to the teeth with it!
what do you want for dinner?

enthusiasm

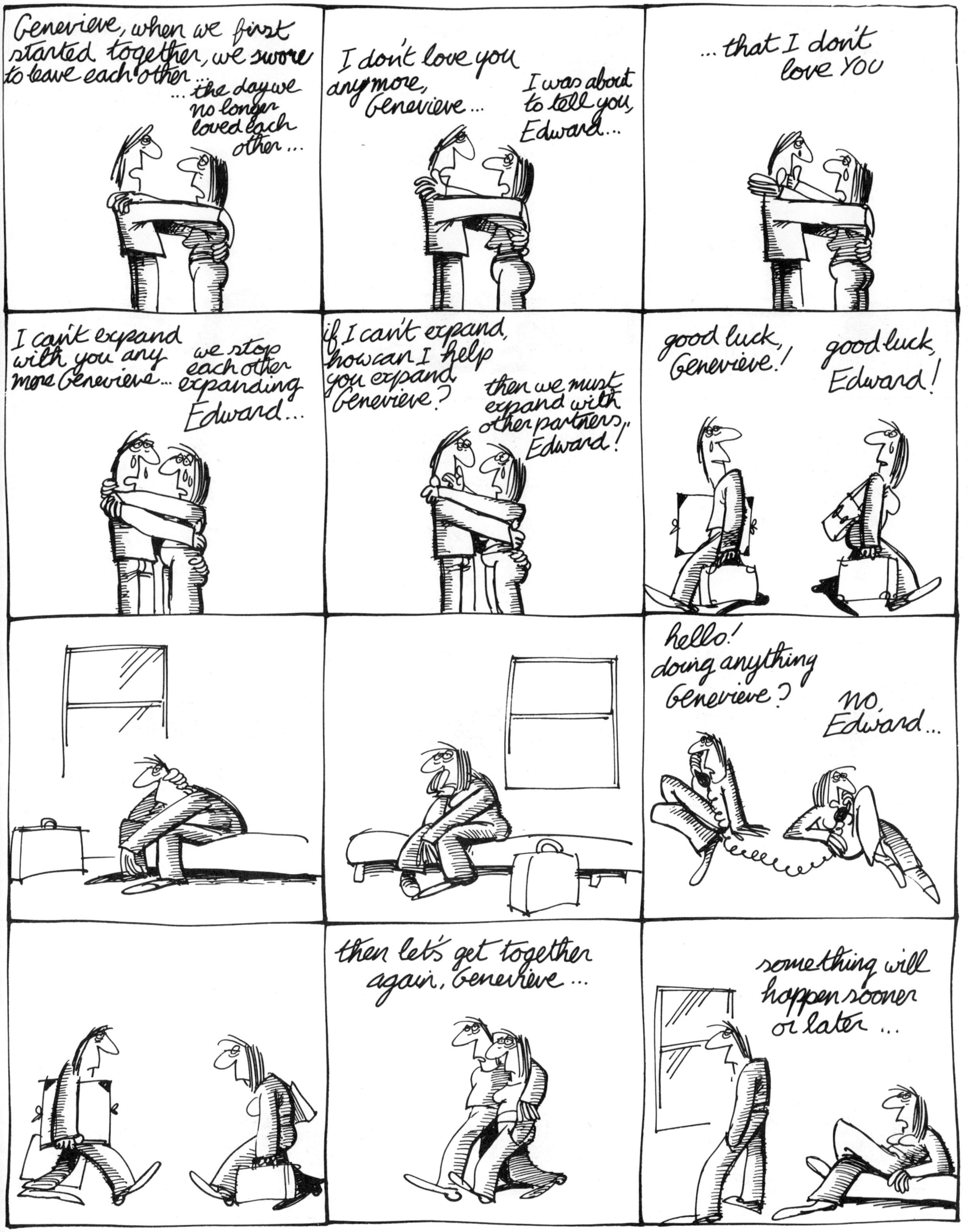

Genevieve, when we first started together, we swore to leave each other
... the day we no longer loved each other ...
I don't love you anymore, Genevieve ...
I was about to tell you, Edward ...
... that I don't love YOU
I can't expand with you any more Genevieve ...
we stop each other expanding Edward ...
if I can't expand, how can I help you expand Genevieve?
then we must expand with other partners, Edward!
good luck, Genevieve!
good luck, Edward!
hello! doing anything Genevieve?
no, Edward ...
then let's get together again, Genevieve ...
something will happen sooner or later ...

interview

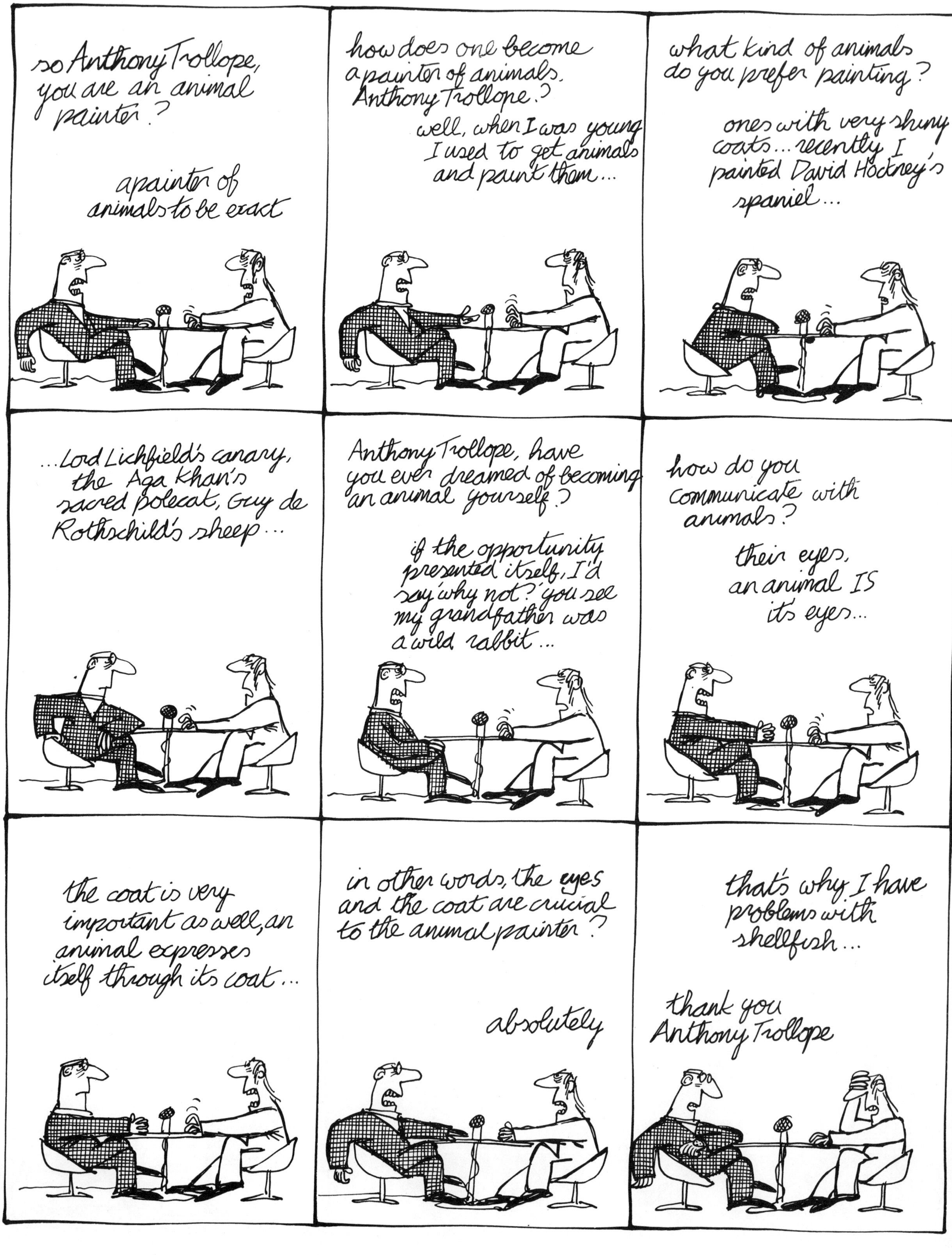
so Anthony Trollope, you are an animal painter?
a painter of animals to be exact
how does one become a painter of animals, Anthony Trollope?
well, when I was young I used to get animals and paint them...
what kind of animals do you prefer painting?
ones with very shiny coats... recently I painted David Hockney's spaniel...
...Lord Lichfield's canary, the Aga Khan's sacred polecat, Guy de Rothschild's sheep...
Anthony Trollope, have you ever dreamed of becoming an animal yourself?
if the opportunity presented itself, I'd say 'why not?' you see my grandfather was a wild rabbit...
how do you communicate with animals?
their eyes, an animal IS its eyes...
the coat is very important as well, an animal expresses itself through its coat...
in other words, the eyes and the coat are crucial to the animal painter?
absolutely
that's why I have problems with shellfish...
thank you Anthony Trollope

hair

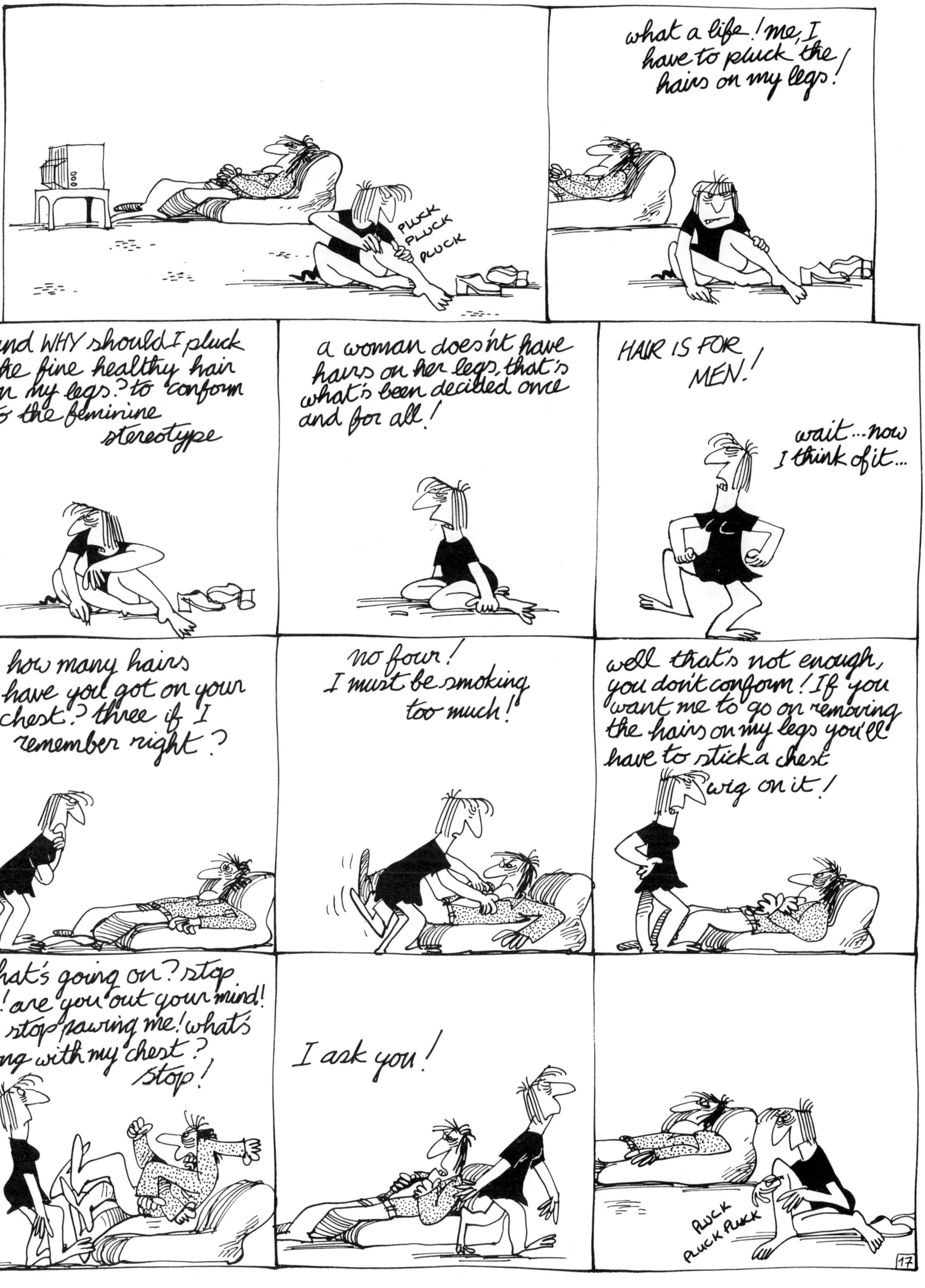
PLUCK
PLUCK
PLUCK
what a life! me, I have to pluck the hairs on my legs!
and WHY should I pluck the fine healthy hair on my legs? to conform to the feminine stereotype
a woman does'nt have hairs on her legs, that's what's been decided once and for all!
HAIR IS FOR MEN!
wait... now I think of it...
how many hairs have you got on your chest? three if I remember right?
no four! I must be smoking too much!
well that's not enough, you don't conform! If you want me to go on removing the hairs on my legs you'll have to stick a chest wig on it!
what's going on? stop it! are you out your mind!
then stop pawing me! what's wrong with my chest? stop!
I ask you!
PLUCK
PLUCK PLUCK

blank title

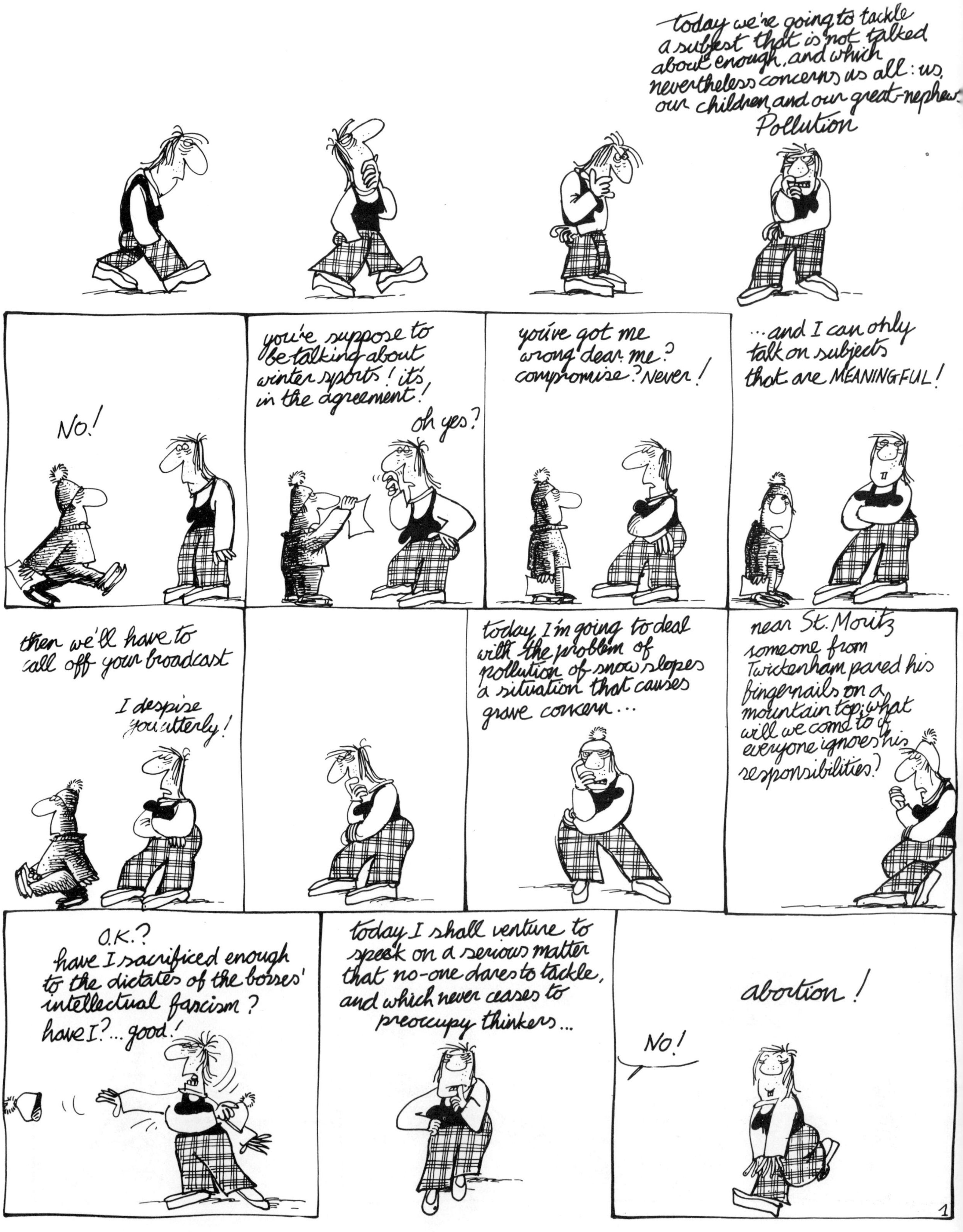
today we're going to tackle a subject that is not talked about enough, and which nevertheless concerns us all: us, our children and our great-nephews
Pollution
No!
you're suppose to be talking about winter sports! it's in the agreement!
oh yes?
you've got me wrong dear me? compromise? Never!
...and I can only talk on subjects that are MEANINGFUL!
then we'll have to call off your broadcast
I despise you utterly!
today I'm going to deal with the problem of pollution of snow slopes a situation that causes grave concern...
near St. Moritz someone from Twickenham pared his fingernails on a mountain top: what will we come to if everyone ignores his responsibilities?
O.K.?
have I sacrificed enough to the dictates of the bosses' intellectual fascism? have I?... good!
today I shall venture to speak on a serious matter that no-one dares to tackle, and which never ceases to preoccupy thinkers...
No!
abortion!

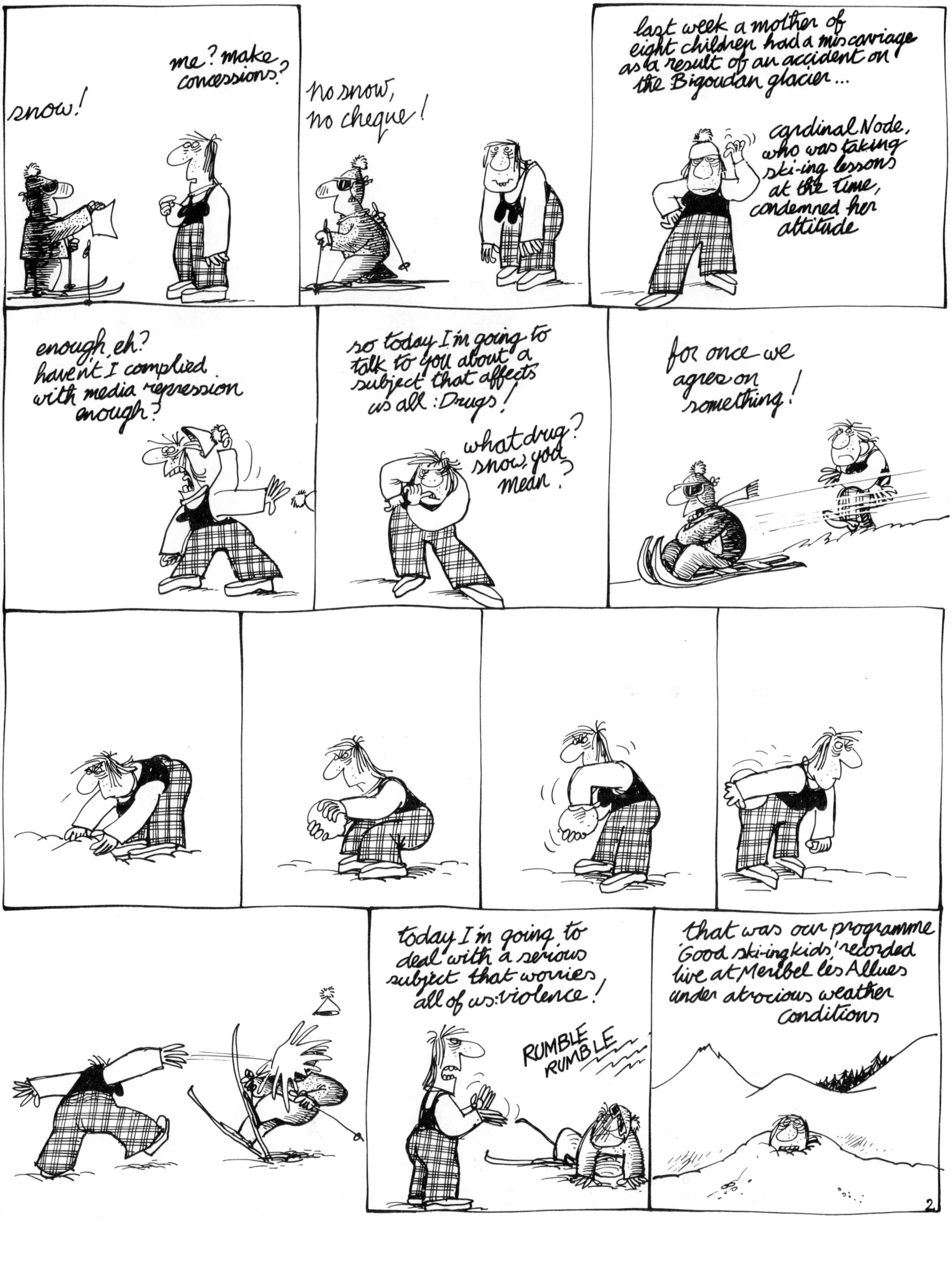
snow!
me? make concessions?
no snow, no cheque!
last week a mother of eight children had a miscarriage as a result of an accident on the Bigoudan glacier ...
cardinal Node, who was taking ski-ing lessons at the time, condemned her attitude
enough, eh? haven't I complied with media repression enough?
so today I'm going to talk to you about a subject that affects us all: Drugs!
what drug? snow, you mean?
for once we agree on something!
today I'm going to deal with a serious subject that worries all of us: violence!
RUMBLE RUMBLE
that was our programme 'Good ski-ing kids' recorded live at Meribel les Allues under atrocious weather conditions

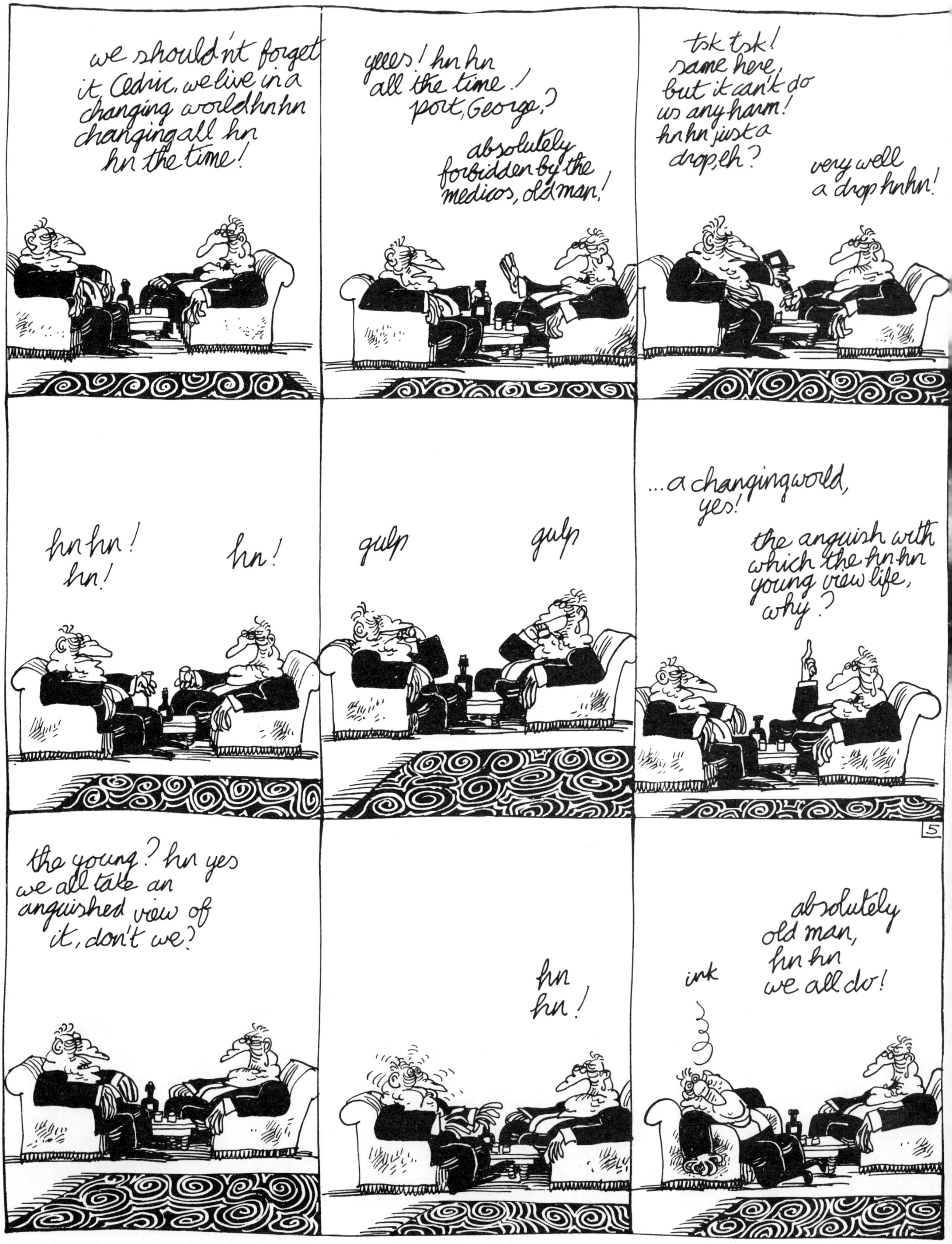
we should'nt forget it Cedric, we live in a changing world hn hn changing all hn hn the time!
yeees! hn hn all the time! port, George?
absolutely forbidden by the medicos, old man!
tsk tsk! same here, but it can't do us any harm! hn hn just a drop, eh?
very well a drop hn hn!
hn hn! hn!
hn!
gulp
gulp
...a changing world, yes!
the anguish with which the hn hn young view life, why?
5
the young? hn yes we all take an anguished view of it, don't we?
hn hn!
ink
absolutely old man, hn hn we all do!

virility

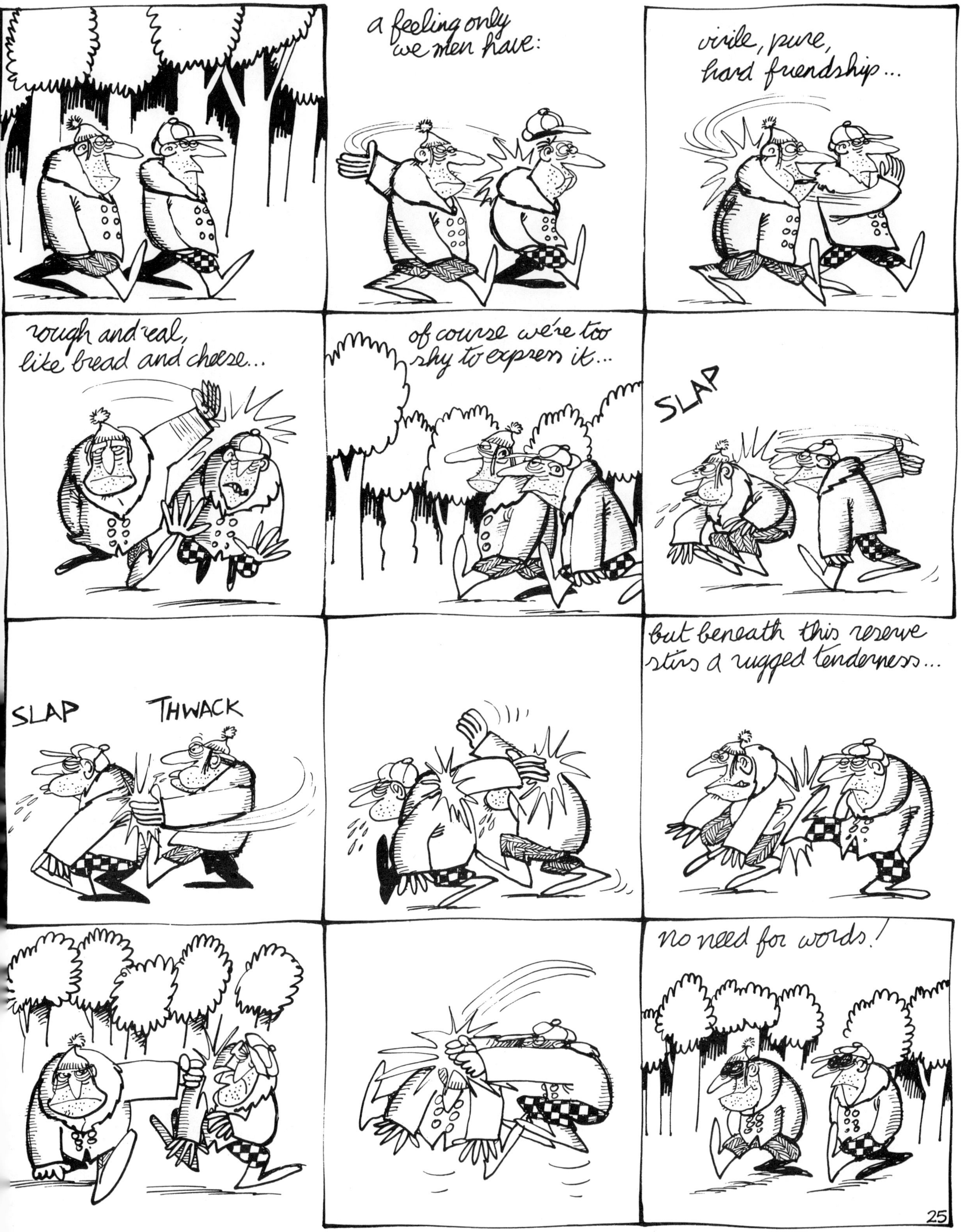
a feeling only we men have:
virile, pure, hard friendship...
rough and real, like bread and cheese...
of course we're too shy to express it...
SLAP
SLAP
THWACK
but beneath this reserve stirs a rugged tenderness...
no need for words!

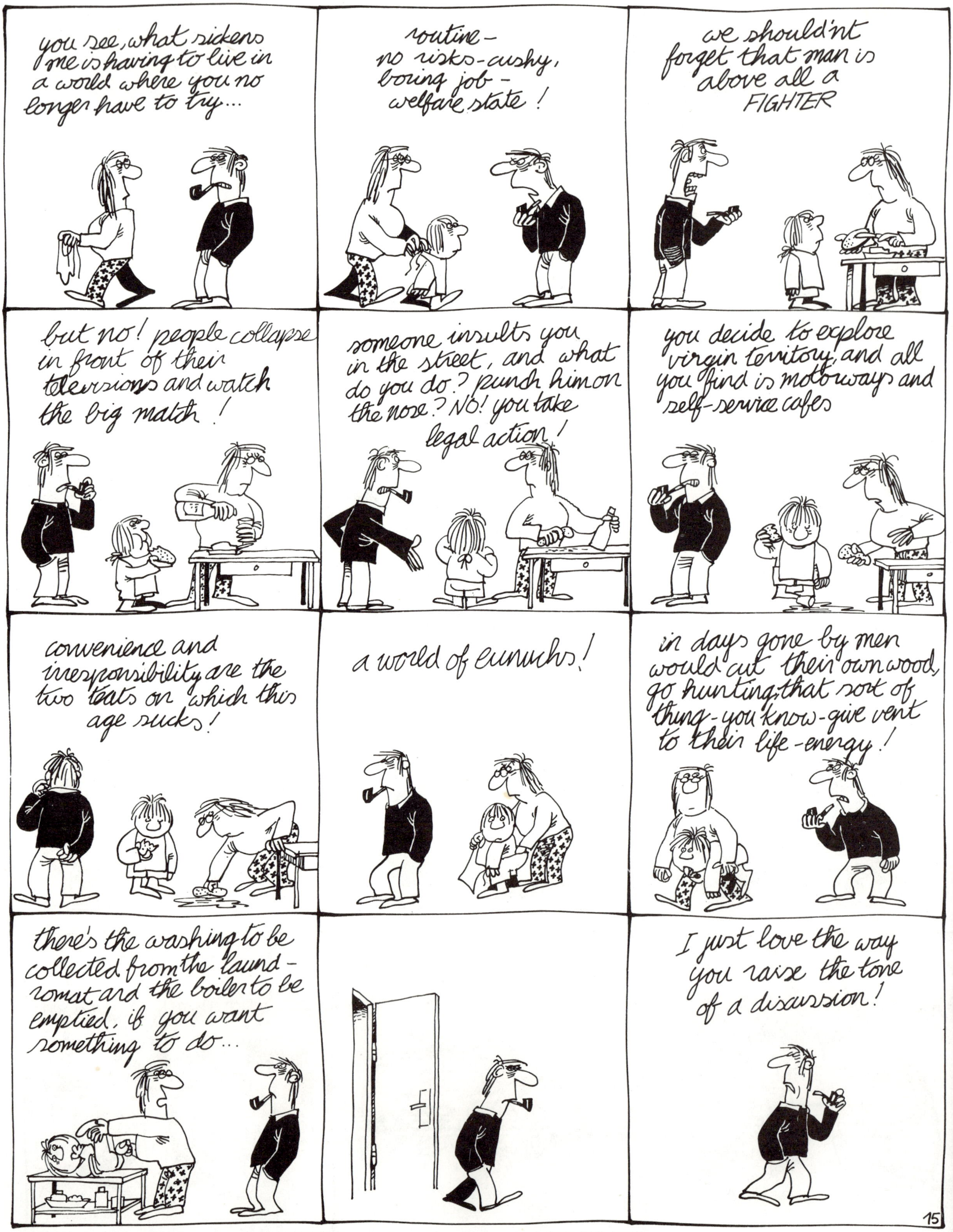
you see, what sickens me is having to live in a world where you no longer have to try...
routine - no risks - cushy, boring job - welfare state!
we shouldn't forget that man is above all a FIGHTER
but no! people collapse in front of their televisions and watch the big match!
someone insults you in the street, and what do you do? punch him on the nose? NO! you take legal action!
you decide to explore virgin territory, and all you find is motorways and self-service cafes
convenience and irresponsibility are the two teats on which this age sucks!
a world of eunuchs!
in days gone by men would cut their own wood, go hunting, that sort of thing - you know - give vent to their life-energy!
there's the washing to be collected from the laundromat and the boiler to be emptied, if you want something to do...
I just love the way you raise the tone of a discussion!

everyday pleasures

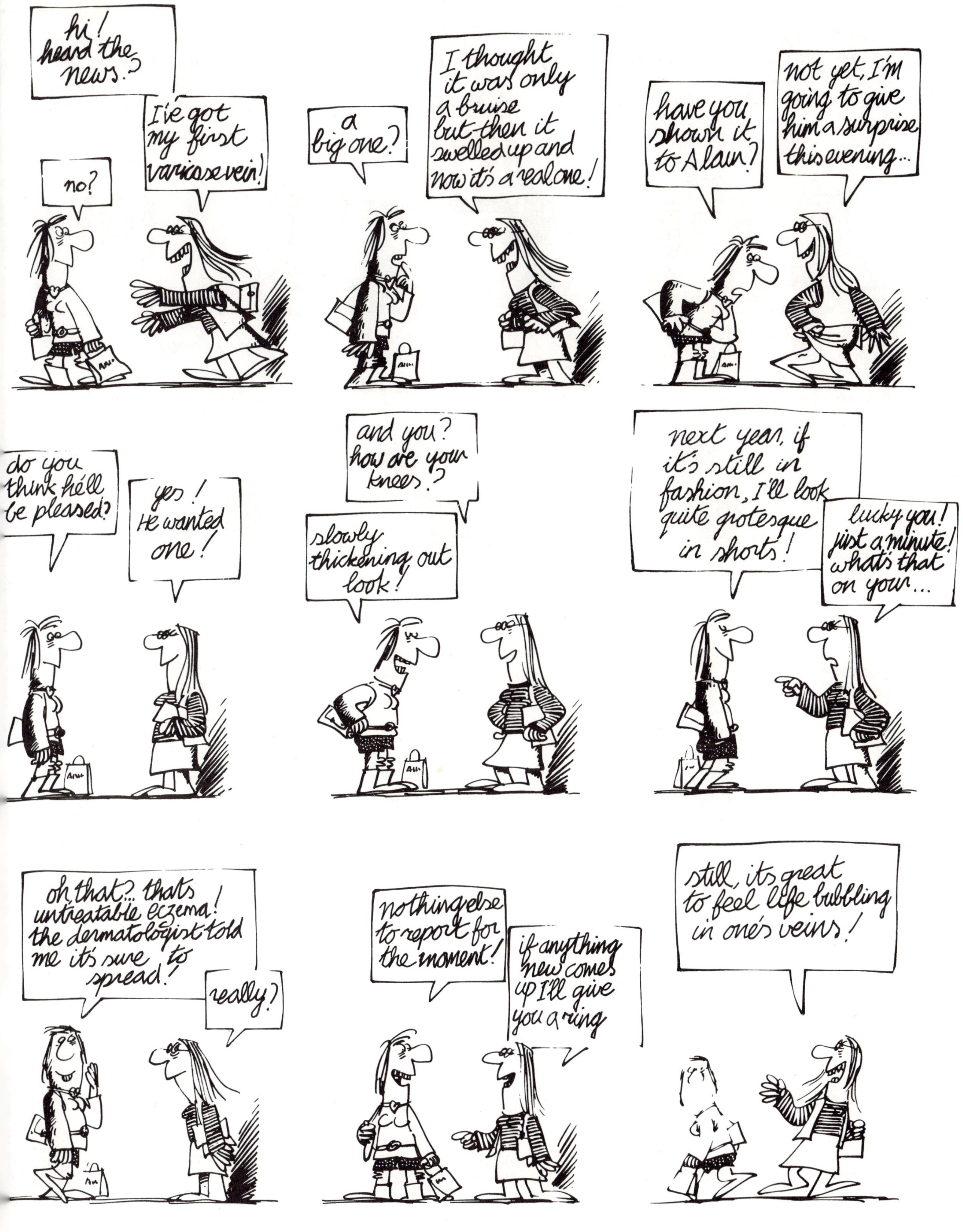
hi! heard the news?
no?
I've got my first varicose vein!
a big one?
I thought it was only a bruise but then it swelled up and now it's a real one!
have you shown it to Alain?
not yet, I'm going to give him a surprise this evening...
do you think he'll be pleased?
yes! He wanted one!
and you? how are your knees?
slowly thickening out look!
next year, if it's still in fashion, I'll look quite grotesque in shorts!
lucky you! just a minute! what's that on your...
oh that?... that's untreatable eczema! the dermatologist told me it's sure to spread!
really?
nothing else to report for the moment!
if anything new comes up I'll give you a ring
still, it's great to feel life bubbling in one's veins!

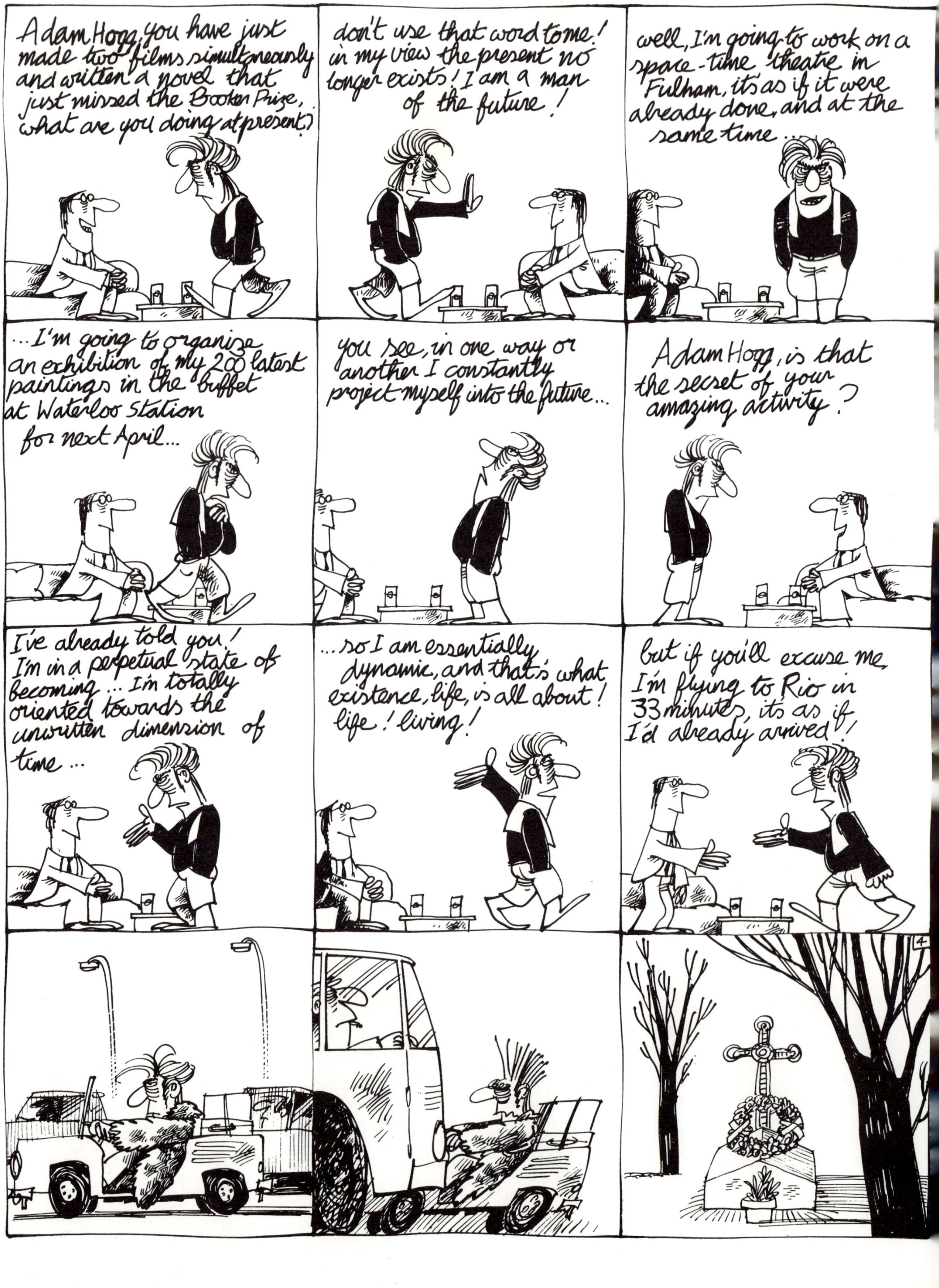
Adam Hogg, you have just made two films simultaneously and written a novel that just missed the Booker Prize, what are you doing at present?
don't use that word to me! in my view the present no longer exists! I am a man of the future!
well, I'm going to work on a space-time theatre in Fulham, it's as if it were already done, and at the same time ...
... I'm going to organize an exhibition of my 200 latest paintings in the buffet at Waterloo Station for next April ...
you see, in one way or another I constantly project myself into the future ...
Adam Hogg, is that the secret of your amazing activity?
I've already told you! I'm in a perpetual state of becoming ... I'm totally oriented towards the unwritten dimension of time ...
... so I am essentially dynamic, and that's what existence, life, is all about! life! living!
but if you'll excuse me, I'm flying to Rio in 33 minutes, it's as if I'd already arrived!

sicut dolor meus . . .

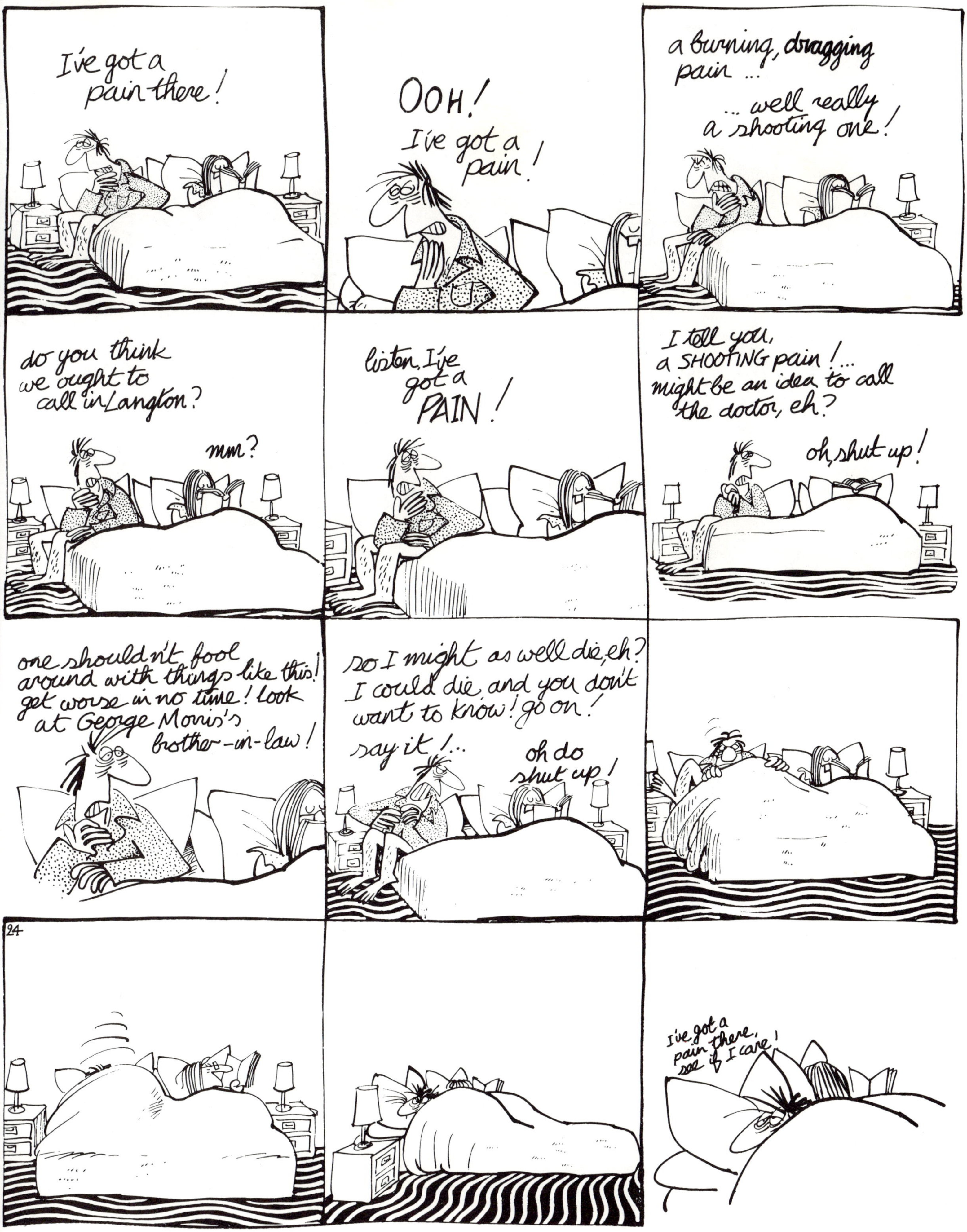

I've got a pain there!
OOH! I've got a pain!
a burning, dragging pain ...
... well really a shooting one!
do you think we ought to call in Langton?
mm?
listen, I've got a PAIN!
I tell you, a SHOOTING pain!... might be an idea to call the doctor, eh?
oh, shut up!
one shouldn't fool around with things like this! get worse in no time! look at George Morris's brother-in-law!
so I might as well die, eh? I could die, and you don't want to know! go on! say it!...
oh do shut up!
I've got a pain there, see if I care!

when I see the lives people put up with, I'm amazed!

just not possible!

take the guy downstairs — every morning, 8:30 sharp, he's making nuts and bolts!

unbelievable!

take my father: forty years in the shoe trade, and what's more he's happy!

unthinkable!

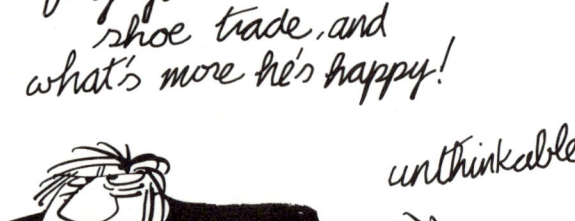

look at my mother! forty five years in pharmaceutical glass!

Insane! insane!

look at Andrew: he not only does an eight hour grind, but he brings his work back

doesn't bear thinking about!

people waste their life, their one and only life! they waste it!

why?

masochists the lot!

23

it sickens me, sometimes it really sickens me

mm

I tell you, if I could find some deal paying a thousand quid a month, you wouldn't see me down at JWT tomorrow!

we're masochists!